KARA'S QUEST

LINDA SHEPHERD

Dear Rhoda,

    Thank you so much for your help to us.
We really appreciate it from the bottom of our
hearts.

                Love,
             Pastor Charlie, Judy, Celeste & Elise
                Aug. 29, 1997

OLIVER
NELSON

THOMAS NELSON PUBLISHERS
Nashville

To my daughter, Laura, who is my brook of joy.
Special thanks to Debbie, Kari, and Amy.

❖

Published in Nashville, Tennessee, by Oliver-Nelson Books, a division of Thomas Nelson, Inc., Publishers, and distributed in Canada by Word Communications, Ltd., Richmond, British Columbia.

This is a work of fiction. The events, settings, and characters are not intended to represent specific events, places, or persons.

Library of Congress Cataloging-in-Publication Data

Shepherd, Linda E., 1957–
    Kara's quest / Linda E. Shepherd.
        p.   cm.
    Summary: A devotional with daily Bible readings and prayers
combined with an account of the various challenges faced by
teenagers, as reflected in the daily life of the fictional Kara Daniels.
    ISBN 0-8407-9680-3
    1. Teenagers—Prayer-books and devotions—English.   2. Christian
life—Juvenile literature.   [1. Prayer books and devotions.
2. Christian life.]   I. Title.
BV4531.2.S534   1993
242′.63—dc20   93–26476
                                                                        CIP
                                                                         AC

Printed in the United States of America.
1 2 3 4 5 6 — 98 97 96 95 94 93

THE BLESSING

*Let us fix our eyes on Jesus, the author and
perfecter of our faith.*—Hebrews 12:2 (NIV)

Sixteen-year-old Kara Daniels's heart pounded as she hobbled
down the school hallway. Her shoulder-length brown hair whipped
in knots, and her mascara streaked like war paint across her face.
Why today? Kara thought with a grimace. Stumbling, she looked
down at her feet. She was wearing only one tennis shoe! It had been
the only one she could find after ransacking her house.

Gasping for breath, she swung open a classroom door. Twenty-five
pairs of eyes shot her with disgust.

Swallowing hard, she tried to speak, "Uh . . . help me. I've lost
my class! I'm supposed to be taking an algebra test."

As the class stared, a buzzing sound jolted Kara into relief. And
she realized she was . . . just dreaming.

She turned off the alarm and snuggled deeper into her pillow.
She had to get up. After all, it was the first day of the new school
year.

Kara pulled herself out of bed, shuddering at the still vivid nightmare. Shuffling to her closet, she thought, *I'll be careful to avoid
trouble this semester. I want my sophomore year to be perfect!*

An hour later, Kara's family gathered around the breakfast table.
Her dad sat beside her, pushing his glasses higher on his nose. He
said, "This school year is sure to get hectic, so to help you get off
to a good start, your mom and I want to give all of you a blessing."

Creasing his freckled forehead, ten-year-old Bryce asked, "A blessing? You mean you want to ask God to help us survive school?"

Mr. Daniels answered, "Not only do we want you to survive, we want you to do it in the spirit of boldness. Your mom and I bless you with the ability to stand up for what you believe, no matter what happens!"

Kara frowned. "That blessing sounds dangerous. Conflict is the last thing I need. I want this to be my best year ever!"

Smiling, Mrs. Daniels sat her steaming coffee on the table. "Kara, I always say, hope for the best, but be ready for anything! Besides, taking a stand for Christ might not be so bad. It could prove to be the adventure of a lifetime."

Eighteen-year-old Matt laughed, raising his orange juice glass into the air. "Here's to adventure. Ready or not, here we come!"

Lord, being open to Your will can sometimes put a person in uncomfortable situations. There's a price to pay for following You, but there's also a reward. Help me remember, running a race is hard work, but the celebration at the finish line will make all of my efforts worth any pain.

Additional Scripture reading: 1 Corinthians 9:24–27

HANGING OUT

Beloved, let us love one another, for love is of
God; and everyone who loves is born of God
and knows God.—1 John 4:7

The school yard of Summitview High vibrated with greetings and bright fall fashions.

Kara and her best friend, Jenni, hung back from the clamor.

Jenni asked, "Kara, are you ready for this?"

"Sort of," Kara answered, glancing in the direction of a group of guys. "There are some things about school I really missed."

Jenni followed Kara's eyes and giggled. "I can't imagine why. We might as well be invisible when it comes to *them*."

Kara nodded, studying a blond athlete. "You're right, but haven't you ever wondered what it would be like to go on a real date?"

Jenni blocked Kara's vision. "Now don't go getting boy crazy or you'll start acting like those brainless cheerleaders over there." Jenni tilted her head. "Look at them. Every time a guy walks by they go gaga."

Kara's eyes swept the giggling girls. "That's not fair, Jenni, the Bible says we should love our neighbors. I wouldn't mind being friends with them."

"I don't think I'd fit in," Jenni observed, "and it would be hard for you to stand up for the truth by yourself." She scrutinized Kara. "I don't want to lose you, and you don't want to get sucked into a situation you can't handle."

"Don't worry about me, Jenni. I took notes when my youth director talked about peer pressure and premarital sex. Besides, those girls won't speak to me anyway." Kara peeked from behind her brown bangs to scan the faces of her classmates.

"That's the way it *has* been," Jenni agreed. "But what would you do if things changed?"

Kara's eyes snapped to Jenni. "Providing you'd still speak to me, I'd like a chance to find out."

Jenni smiled. "Maybe, but only if I could join you. A little adventure might be fun," she admitted.

Lord, You know I don't want to be a Christian snob. Yet, I know You want me to be careful with whom I hang out. Give me balance and wisdom in this area. Open the relationships that are right for me, and close the ones that aren't. Help me be a good friend and share You with others.

Additional Scripture reading: Mark 12:28–34

❖

SUDDEN STAND

In the world you will have tribulation; but
be of good cheer, I have overcome the world.
—John 16:33

Kara caught Jenni's eye, then darted a look at her watch as if to say, *Hang in there. It's almost over!* Jenni nodded, her smile almost hiding her braces. Ten more minutes and they'd be free!

Kara sighed, glad the day had passed without incident. She tapped her pen on her school desk. *Will this social studies class ever end?* Pushing her drooping curls across her neck, she stole another peek at Jenni.

Oh, where is that bell? Kara frowned. *This first day's gone well, almost too well. I've got to get out of here before something happens.*

The teacher's voice grabbed Kara's attention. Mr. Thomas closed his workbook and sat on the edge of his desk. He said, "You know, class, social studies is about how people live. To explore today's generation, I will occasionally lead class discussions. Today's topic is premarital sex. I'd like you to raise your hand if you think it's okay to have sex before marriage."

A flush crept across Kara's cheeks. Her eyes swept the room. One by one, her classmates lifted their hands, giving the effect of slow-popping corn. Shooting a quick glance at Jenni, Kara noticed her hands remained planted on her desk. Kara's heart skipped a beat, and she prayed, *Jesus, HELP! Jenni and I are the only ones not raising our hands!*

Kara melted into her chair. *This is humiliating! Sometimes I think being a Christian is hard. Maybe too hard. You gotta help me, Jesus. Show me what to do.*

Even when I'm not prepared, help me boldly stand up for what I believe. Even if others laugh, let me know it's important to be a candle in a dark room. In those lonely moments, let me feel Your hand resting on my shoulder as if to say, "Stand tall. I am with you, and I have overcome the world."

Additional Scripture reading: 2 Timothy 1:3–12

UNDERCOVER CHRISTIAN

For our light affliction, which is but for a
moment, is working for us a far more
exceeding and eternal weight of glory.
—2 Corinthians 4:17

Jack Raymond, a good-looking football player, sat in the desk behind Kara's. Poking Kara with his pen, he quipped, "Hey, Kara, I was thinking of asking you out, but I've just changed my mind."

The class roared with laughter as Kara's flush deepened.

Nancy Adams flung her jet black hair behind her back and cracked, "What's the matter? Are you and Jenni some kind of puritans?"

"Give me a break, Nancy! It's just that the Bible teaches—"

"The Bible!" Jack grimaced, rolling his eyes. "Wow, you're more out of it than I thought! We've got some kind of nut case here!"

Kara opened her mouth to respond, but the clang of the bell sent her classmates into a wild, whooping scramble.

Kara sat frozen in her chair until Jenni tugged her arm. "Come on, Kara, let's get out of here."

Kara stood shakily. "Well, I guess that scene ruined our school year *and* our witness."

Jenni shrugged and guided Kara toward the hall. "You never know, maybe someone was listening and . . ."

"Hey, Kara, Jenni. Wait up!" a voice called from behind.

Kara and Jenni turned to peer into Dee Ann Miller's baby blue eyes. Dee Ann gushed, "I just want to tell you I admire you two for standing up to the class. You see, I'm a Christian, too."

Jenni's eyes widened. "But you raised your hand!"

"I know, I *had* to. I'm trying out for the cheerleading squad tomorrow. Hey, I've got to run. Jack's waiting for me by my locker. See ya," Dee Ann giggled as she tossed her long blond hair and disappeared into the crowded hallway.

You are my Lord and King! Of You, I never want to be ashamed! Always remind me the cost of following You is worth any price. For instead of a timid spirit, You've given me power, love, and self-discipline. May others know You are mine and I am Yours.

Additional Scripture reading: 2 Corinthians 4:1–9

❖

THE CONFRONTATION

It is written: "I believed; therefore I have spoken." With that same spirit of faith we also believe and therefore speak.—2 Corinthians 4:13 (NIV)

Kara and Jenni rounded the hall corner, entering a sea of bobbing faces. "Oh, great!" Kara said, reddening. "Dee Ann and Jack are standing next to our lockers."

Wrinkling her brow, Jenni said, "I think I feel a confrontation coming on. There's no way to duck out."

A sneer erupted on Jack's face when he caught sight of the forlorn pair. He said, "Looky here! If it isn't the *Moral Minority* of Summitview High!"

Kara jerked open the door to her locker, warning, "Lay off, Jack! I'm not in the mood for your crudeness."

Jack persisted, "At least answer a question for me."

"That depends," Kara replied, rummaging for her books.

"I want to know where you get off telling others how to live their lives! You know, you shouldn't try to force your stupid views on everyone else," Jack taunted.

Whirling around, Kara said, "Who says I'm forcing my views on anyone? At least I was honest about what I believe, unlike some people in class." Kara darted a look at Dee Ann. "But now that you mention it, I do think premarital sex is . . . well . . . asking for trouble."

"Hey, not if you're careful," Jack replied with a smug grin. "We learned all about that stuff in grade school. I don't get what your beef is. And don't try to pull that Bible stuff on me either."

Kara closed her locker door. "Jack, it's just I believe you should wait for that special person, that person you are going to spend the rest of your life with." Kara warned, "Today, you have to consider things like venereal diseases, AIDS, unwanted pregnancies, and abortions."

As she tilted her head, Dee Ann's golden hair rippled down her back. Her face clouded in a pout, and she asked, "Kara, how are you going to know when you've met that *special person* as you call it?"

"Yeah, why not play the field and find out what you really like?" Jack agreed, pulling Dee Ann close.

Hugging her books, Kara answered, "If you really liked someone, you'd be willing to wait. You'd respect that person. Don't you realize the system encourages us to have sex because it's big business? Have you ever heard the health teacher say we've got the right to say no?"

Kara shook her head, answering her own question. "I haven't. We're told only to *be safe*. The safest thing you can do is wait. When you've waited for that special person in marriage, then . . . it would be . . . well, worth it."

Jack interrupted, "Kara, stop preaching!" He squeezed Dee Ann and said, "Hey, Babe, I can't take any more of this kind of talk. We're outta here."

I pray for that special person You planned for me since the beginning of time. Even though we may have yet to meet, help us grow together in You. Protect us from the lies of the world, and shelter us with Your shield of truth. Don't let us slip into sexual sin, but help us stay pure as a gift to You and each other.

Additional Scripture reading: Galatians 6:1–10

❖

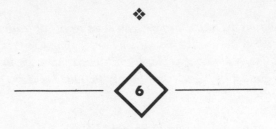

SEEDLINGS

I planted, Apollos watered, but God gave the increase.—1 Corinthians 3:6

Kara and Jenni watched Jack and Dee Ann wander down the hall, arm in arm. Sighing, Kara slumped against her locker and asked, "Do you think they were listening?"

Jenni studied the tile beneath her feet. "It's hard to say. Jack seems to have made up his mind."

Hanging her head, Kara deflated like a nail-punctured tire. She said, "I guess it was worth a try. But they'll probably never speak to me again. Me and my big mouth."

As the couple disappeared around the corner, Jenni looked up. "Kara, don't be so hard on yourself. You did the right thing. Who knows? You may have planted a seed!"

"A seed? What are you talking about?"

"You gave them something to think about. Maybe those thoughts will germinate."

"Well, I hope they could hear over all those hormones roaring in their ears."

"There wouldn't be a problem if teenagers' hormones roared only in their *ears!*" Jenni said with a laugh, patting Kara's shoulder.

"But if it'd help you feel better, I'm almost positive Dee Ann was listening. Perhaps underneath that know-it-all smile, she understood exactly where you were coming from."

"I hope you're right, Jenni. I really do. I'd hate to see Dee Ann and Jack get caught in the sex trap. It's too dangerous."

Jenni nodded in agreement. "Me, too, Kara. Me, too."

Lord, help me be like a farmer who sows words of truth into good soil. Let me realize a seed will never sprout if it is never planted. Teach me how to plant, and teach me when to water. I give my garden of friends and family to You. Let them grow into a harvest of faith!

Additional Scripture reading: Luke 8:5–17

❖

DATE WRONG

Two are better than one. . . .
For if they fall, one will lift up his companion.
But woe to him who is alone when he falls,
For he has no one to help him up.
      —Ecclesiastes 4:9–10

Kara scurried to the girls' locker room, searching for her forgotten gym bag. She didn't need ripe gym clothes for Monday morning's class!

At the dressing room door, she paused, listening to the sound of a muffled noise. *What's that?* she wondered.

She froze in the doorway, barely breathing. A steady drip echoed from the showers while a smothered sob seeped from behind a closed partition.

"Hello?" Kara's voice echoed off the lockers. "Can I help you?" Kara tiptoed to the partition and confided, "It's me, Kara Daniels. Are you okay in there?"

A voice muttered, "Go away! You're the last person I want to talk to!"

Kara's eyes widened. She replied, "Dee Ann! Is that you?"

The partition creaked open, revealing a pale, mascara-stained face.

Kara gasped. "Dee Ann! What's wrong?"

Rising from her hideout, Dee Ann crumpled onto a nearby bench. "I . . . I ju . . . just can't stop crying," she sobbed. "I . . . I . . . feel so *dirty*. Oh, why couldn't I be like you, Kara?"

"Be like *me?*" Kara exclaimed, encircling Dee Ann with her arms. "Why, Dee Ann, you're one of the most popular girls in school. You just made the cheerleading squad! All the guys love you! They hardly speak to me unless they call me *Church Lady* first."

"That's just it!" Dee Ann sniffed. "Everyone knows where you stand. They respect that. Me? Everyone expects me to go along with the crowd. They won't even listen when I say no."

Kara's heart skipped a beat. She asked, "Dee Ann? What do you mean? Did someone force you to do something against your will?"

Dee Ann's lip trembled. "I told Jack no, but he wouldn't listen. We'd been drinking. I told him I wasn't sure . . ." Dee Ann buried her face in her hands. "I feel so dirty and used!"

Kara gasped. She stuttered, "Do . . . do you mean Jack *raped* you? Oh, Dee Ann!"

"It's all my fault." Dee Ann sighed. "I should have made it clear from the beginning. If only I had raised my hand that day in class, like you did. Then Jack would have known how I felt."

"Dee Ann!" Kara cried, stamping her foot. "Jack had no right! He was wrong!"

A tear dripped off the end of Dee Ann's nose. "I know. But I wish I hadn't put myself into that situation! I couldn't control what happened." Dee Ann's voice choked with emotion. "It was horrible, just *horrible!*"

Let me be the kind of friend others can lean on as a loving shoulder. If I see others fallen in my path, help me not to step over them, but teach me how to reach down and pull them up without falling.

Additional Scripture reading: 2 Corinthians 4:7–12

❖

CHOICE GONE WRONG!

But You have seen, for You observe
　　trouble and grief,
To repay it by Your hand.
The helpless commits himself to
　　You.—Psalm 10:14

Tears filled Kara's eyes, and she hugged Dee Ann. "Have you told anyone?"

"No, I'm too ashamed," Dee Ann said, shriveling like a withered rose. Her face twisted with pain. "You're the only person who knows."

Kara blinked, then encouraged, "Dee Ann, I think you should at least tell your parents."

Dee Ann whispered, "You don't understand. My parents put a lot of pressure on me not to embarrass them." Dee Ann shivered. "I've failed them! Can't you see that?"

"No, I don't see," Kara blazed. "You put yourself in a dangerous situation, but Jack should have respected you when you said no!" Kara struck the bench with her fist. "Speaking of Jack, what does he say now?"

"That's the worst part," Dee Ann confided as the shower heads drummed their drip. "When it was all over, he just laughed." A tear glided down her cheek. "He just drove me home and left without even saying good-bye." Dee Ann sighed. "Now my whole life is *ruined!*"

"That's not true, Dee Ann!" Kara exclaimed. "God will get you through this. You'll see."

Dee Ann's face flecked with blotches. "Why would God want to help me? I've failed *Him*, too!"

"Dee Ann, we all make mistakes!" Kara consoled. She stroked Dee Ann's hair. "God loves you, even if you put yourself in a dangerous situation! He wants to comfort you. He doesn't offer you anger. He offers only love and forgiveness. All you have to do is to accept them."

"I was thinking of sleeping with Jack. Isn't God punishing me for *that?*"

Kara captured Dee Ann's eyes with compassion. "*No*, that's not the loving God I know.

"He gives us freedom to make choices. We have to live with the results of those choices. In your case, you made some wrong choices. But even so, Jack chose to hurt you." Kara paused. "Let God get you through this. He's on your side!"

Managing a little smile, Dee Ann said, "Thanks, Kara."

"But listen," Kara continued, "I think you should talk to an adult. If you can't talk to your folks or tell the police, maybe you could call the rape crisis number in the newspaper. Or maybe you could talk to the school counselor—"

Shaking her head, Dee Ann blurted, "No, I don't want anyone to know! It might get back to my parents."

"But, Dee Ann, you need more help than I can give you. You might need to be treated for a venereal disease or uh . . . perhaps you should find out if you're preg—"

"NO!"

Kara extended her hand toward Dee Ann's. "Well, I can't

make you get help. But I'm here for you. Let me know if I can do anything."

"I will," Dee Ann said, grasping Kara's fingers. "Thanks."

Jesus, I thank You for being full of compassion. It doesn't even matter if I'm the one to blame for my pain or not; You're always there for me. Help me reflect this kind of compassion to my friends and family. Help me to be an I-hurt-with-you Christian, who hands out hugs instead of shrugs.

Additional Scripture reading: Psalm 145:1–21

FRIENDS FOREVER?

A talebearer reveals secrets,
But he who is of a faithful spirit conceals
a matter.—Proverbs 11:13

When Kara returned from the gym, she found a scowling Jenni waiting by the water fountain. "What took you so long, Kara?" Jenni pouted. "Matt left half an hour ago. Now we'll have to walk home."

Kara knew how disappointed Jenni was at the prospect of missing a ride with Matt. Jenni had been not so secretly in love with him since second grade.

Studying her slightly plump friend, Kara remembered the giggly school bus rides that had carried them through the years. But now that Matt drove a car, the bus rides had turned into a car pool, complete with little brother Bryce.

Although the car pool provided the perfect opportunity for Jenni to vie for Matt's attention, she remained unnoticed. While others admired Jenni's deep blue eyes highlighting her delicate oval face, Matt considered Jenni a sister, a transparent one at that.

Kara put her arm around her friend as they strolled into the afternoon sunshine. She blinked against the brightness. "Sorry, Jen. I found Dee Ann crying in the locker room, and I stopped to talk to her."

"What happened? Did she and Jack break up?" Jenni asked, her eyes wide with curiosity.

"I guess so," Kara responded, "but I really can't talk about it."

Jenni swung her books over one hip and stared at her friend. "Kara, you've never shut me out before. Why can't you tell me what happened? We're still best friends, aren't we?"

"Of course, but . . ." Kara changed the subject. "Are you still planning to try out for Show Choir?"

Jenni waved her sheet music in the air. "Got music, will practice!" she declared.

With a flourish, Jenni stepped ahead of Kara, twirling to face her friend. "Now, don't go changing the subject. Why can't you tell me what happened with Dee Ann?" Jenni asked. "I don't like being left out. Our friendship is important to me . . . very important."

"Our friendship is important to me, too. I'm not trying to hurt you. I just won't be a gossip."

Jenni frowned. "Kara, I don't want us to drift apart." She lowered her eyes. "Not only are you my best friend, you're my only friend. I'd just *die* without you."

Furrowing her brows, Kara said, "Jenni, you're allowed to have other friends, you know."

Swinging around, Jenni faced the hot afternoon breeze that tangled through her golden curls. "We've been buds for so long, I just wouldn't know how to start a new friendship."

"Just be yourself, Jenni. That's all you'd need to do." Kara patted Jenni's shoulder. "Besides, I'll always be around for you. You'll see."

Teach me not only how to have friends but how to be a friend.
And help me remember I'm never alone, no matter how lonely I

might feel. Teach me Your love and friendship for me are real.
Thank You for Your faithfulness to me.

Additional Scripture reading: Ephesians 4:21–32

❖

LOCKER
LOCKHEADS

All who desire to live godly in Christ Jesus
will suffer persecution.—2 Timothy 3:12

Kara's Monday morning arrived too soon. As she and Jenni made
their way through swirls of teenagers, Jenni stopped, warning Kara
with a touch.

"Jen, what is it?" Kara probed, facing her friend. She followed
Jenni's eyes in the direction of their lockers. "Oh . . . it's *them!*"
Kara frowned.

Jenni threw a concerned look at Kara. "Promise me no matter
what happens, you'll ignore them!" Jenni begged.

Rosy color tinged Kara's cheeks. "I'll try, Jen, but those guys
are really starting to get to me."

As the girls approached, a trio of boys began to swear like sailors.

Kara's jaw tightened. She whispered to Jenni, "It's as if they
want me to lose my temper."

Jenni nodded, while the boys oinked like pigs.

Kara's eyes flashed fire. "What's that supposed to mean?"

The guys nudged each other. Rodger Tracey called out, "That's
for Jenni to figure out."

Kara whispered to Jenni through gritted teeth, "Pay no attention to them."

Turning to open her locker, Kara felt hot breath tickle the back of her neck. Reaching to brush it away, she reeled to face a freckle-faced Rodger.

"What do you want?" Kara demanded, backing into her open locker.

"I just want to see what a virgin looks like up close," Rodger said with a smirk, pushing his straight black hair out of his eyes.

Stamping her foot, Kara growled, "Look, Rodger, I'm getting tired of you guys bugging us. Leave us alone. And while you're at it, watch your language. We're getting really tired of your foul mouths."

"Oh, is that so?" Rodger sneered. "If our language bothers you, I'll do better . . . I'll really gall you." Cupping his hand, he whispered into Kara's ear. Kara reddened. She scooped up her books and slammed the door of her locker, pushing Rodger aside.

Jesus, Kara prayed while she retreated, *I really need Your help. Show me how to deal with this Rodger character. I know You love him, even though I don't see how.*

Jesus, show me how to love my neighbor despite his spite. I know Your love would make me not a victim but a testimony of Your forgiveness. Because Your love is bold and daring, teach me how to show Your love without faltering.

Additional Scripture reading: James 1:19–21

NEW
FRIENDS

A man who has friends must himself be friendly,
But there is a friend who sticks closer than a
brother.—Proverbs 18:24

Kara scanned the noisy cafeteria looking for Jenni. Feeling a hand on her shoulder, she turned to the warm glow of Dee Ann's eyes.

"Kara, you didn't tell anyone about our conversation the other day, did you?" Dee Ann asked, her eyes pleading desperation.

"No," Kara answered. "I felt it was too . . . personal . . . to share with anyone."

"Not even Jenni?" Dee Ann asked, arching her eyebrows.

"No, it just didn't feel right," Kara admitted.

Dee Ann picked up a tray. "Thanks, Kara. It feels good to have a friend I can trust. How about joining my friends for lunch?"

"Me?" Kara almost dropped her books. "Are you sure I'd be welcome?"

"You are if you're with me," Dee Ann said, laughing.

Kara balanced her books and reached for a tray, her head spinning. Dee Ann's friends were the most popular girls in school. *Being friends with them could mean attention and maybe even,* Kara dared to hope, *a boyfriend.*

"Sure," Kara replied, trying to hide her enthusiasm under a mask of composure.

When the girls reached the table, the cheerleaders exchanged glances.

"Kara's joining us today," Dee Ann announced.

Kara slid into a seat next to Todd James, the school's most gorgeous athlete. Her heart pounded as he studied her with a grin.

Todd said, "You're Matt's sister, aren't you?"

Melting under his gaze, Kara managed a nod. She couldn't help noticing the warm depth of his aqua eyes beneath his blond hair.

"I'm glad you joined us," Todd said, gleaming a smile of perfect white teeth. "I've always thought you seemed like someone I'd like to know."

Blushing, Kara squeaked, "Thanks."

As Kara became caught in the laughter of her companions, a hush fell over the table.

Kara looked up into Jenni's frown.

"Is this seat taken?" Jenni asked.

Before Kara could answer, Brooke Kelly, a beautiful brunette interrupted, "Sorry, it's saved."

Studying her half-eaten hamburger, Kara avoided Jenni's eyes. She couldn't leave now, could she?

Kara watched as Jenni went to sit alone at a table across the room. *Oh, Jenni,* Kara thought, *I'm sorry to hurt you. If only you could understand. I'll make it up to you. You'll see.*

Lord, there is enough hurt in this world without me adding to it. Help me to be not a stumbling block to others but a help. Help me heal hurts, not cause them. But if I should hurt another, help me right the wrong with Your love.

Additional Scripture reading: 1 Corinthians 1:1–10

BEGINNINGS AND ENDINGS

The righteous should choose his
friends carefully,
For the way of the wicked leads them
astray.—Proverbs 12:26

"Who wants to stop at McGuffy's for a cheeseburger fix?" Matt asked his passengers who were jiving to the beat of his latest Carman tape.

Bryce sang out, "I do! I do!"

"I'm not hungry," Jenni interrupted. "If you don't mind, I'd like to go home."

Bryce batted his red hair out of his eyes. "Since when have you ever turned down a cheeseburger, Jen?"

Jenni responded by staring out the window, her jaw jutting in anger.

Kara pressed against Jenni's resentment. "I'm sorry, Jen. It happened so fast, I didn't know what to do. I never meant to hurt you."

"Fast!" Jenni retorted, "That's a good way to describe your new friends."

"They weren't having an orgy, Jenni, just lunch. And I don't think it's fair of you to make those kinds of judgments."

Jenni blurted, "Since I'm not welcome, I guess I'll never know if my judgments are fair or not."

Matt interrupted, "You made some new friends, Kara? Who?"

"Todd James and the cheerleader snips," Jenni snapped.

Kara frosted. Matt's blue eyes questioned her reflection in the rearview mirror. "Todd James?" he asked. "Kara, he's got quite a reputation. What are you doing hanging out with him?"

Kara tried to speak through alternating waves of embarrassment and anger. "He's just a friend, Matt. We're not going out or anything. Besides, he seems like a nice guy."

Matt pulled his red car in front of Jenni's house. Jenni announced, "Don't worry about picking me up tomorrow. This car pool seems a little too crowded lately." She got out and slammed the car door.

Matt ran his fingers through his dark curls. "What's all this about?"

"She's overreacting!" Kara declared. "All I did was have lunch with Dee Ann Miller and her friends. Hasn't anyone ever heard of witnessing? How's a person ever going to share her faith if she never breaks out of her circle of friends?"

Bryce asked, "Well, why is Jenni so mad? Was she left out?"

Dropping her voice, Kara said, "Yes."

"That's the problem, Kara," Matt observed. "Even Jesus sent His disciples out two by two. You can't expect to stand up to a crowd like Todd's friends alone. It's too dangerous."

"What do you mean?" Kara asked.

"Well, what if Todd asked you out? You might be putting yourself in a situation that could be too hot for even a nice Christian girl like you to handle."

Bring me a partner who shares my faith to help me face the world. Help us team together and stand strong. But even when there is no one standing by my side, help me remember You are there. Help me stand for You as You stand by me.

Additional Scripture reading: Proverbs 4:13–19

STEPPING OUT

Let love be without hypocrisy. Abhor what is
evil. Cling to what is good.—Romans 12:9

Kara stormed to her room. How she hated Matt's big brother
lectures—especially this one. Slamming her bedroom door, Kara
stared at her reflection in the mirror. *Why did things always have
to be so complicated?* she asked herself.

She had never meant to hurt Jenni. It had just happened. Besides,
why was everyone so down about her new friends? They couldn't
be that bad, could they? After all, perhaps she could help them,
like she had helped Dee Ann in the locker room.

I can't be a Christian snob, can I? Kara reasoned.

Kara imagined Todd's image in the mirror superimposed over
her own. She pantomimed, "I'm sorry, Todd, but I'm a Christian.
I'm too good to talk to the likes of you. So," Kara stuck out her
tongue, "get lost!"

Glaring into her brown eyes, Kara thought *No, that kind of attitude stinks. Even Jesus wouldn't approve.*

The ringing of the telephone jarred her thoughts. Bryce called
from below, "Kara, it's for you. It's that Dee Ann girl."

Kara bounced down the stairs and grabbed the receiver from
Bryce, who whined, "Can I listen?"

"Not a chance," Kara replied, shoving him into the kitchen and
shutting the door behind him. She could hear Bryce exciting the
dog into yapping frenzy to spite her attempt at privacy.

Putting a hand over one ear and the receiver to the other, Kara
asked, "Dee Ann, what's up?"

Dee Ann's voice radiated over the line. "Some of the girls and I are meeting at Eatza My Pizza tonight to celebrate my birthday. I thought you might like to come."

Kara hesitated. *It wouldn't be fair to say no,* she thought. *Dee Ann's a Christian! With her backup, I couldn't possibly be alone in standing for my faith. Could I?*

"Sure, Dee Ann, seven o'clock? I'll get Matt to drive me."

Dee Ann giggled. "Great! Oh, you might want to wear something hot. You never know who you might meet. See you there!"

Sometimes, Lord, it's so hard to know right from wrong. Give me wisdom and help me sidestep any traps the Enemy is setting for me. Help me overcome, no matter what comes my way. I want to stay true to You.

Additional Scripture reading: 2 Timothy 2:22–24

❖

14

SEX APPEAL

———

I also want women to dress modestly, with decency and propriety.—1 Timothy 2:9 (NIV)

Kara wiggled into her black satin T-strapped camisole, the one she normally wore under her chiffon party blouse. She highlighted her cheekbones with her blush and gave her eyelashes an extra touch of mascara. She stepped back to admire the effect. *Is this hot enough?*

Her figure was flattered in her almost-too-tight black jeans. A couple of days ago, she had almost discarded them as too small, but tonight, they were perfect.

Grabbing her sweater, Kara called to Matt. "I'm ready when you are."

As she slinked into the front seat, Matt eyed her curiously. "Ahhh, Kara, you look different tonight."

"Oh?" Kara said, pleased he had noticed.

"Are you trying to impress your new friends?" Matt asked.

Kara frowned. "What do you mean?"

"Well, your makeup, your clothes. That look is not your style."

"My style?" Kara asked.

"Yeah," Matt said with a nod. "You usually look . . . uh . . . wholesome. But tonight, you look like a . . . a tease."

Bristling with anger, Kara said, "Thanks for the compliment."

Matt continued, "You didn't say. Is Todd going to be at Dee Ann's party? Are you dressed this way for him?"

"How should I know?" Kara retorted. "Besides, I don't see what the big deal is."

Matt's brakes whined to a stop in the Eatza My Pizza parking lot. "Well, just remember, the kind of fish you catch depends on the bait you use. With the kind of bait you're using tonight, you might land a shark."

Matt turned and looked at his sister. "What would you do with a shark?"

Kara slipped into her black sweater bordered with lacy pink flowers and flipped her hair from beneath the collar. "Don't worry, Matt. I won't do anything *stupid*. Besides, *all* the girls dress this way. It's no big deal."

"Maybe not to you and your new friends. But, well, when a guy sees a girl dressed in a . . . a way he thinks is provocative—well, he has . . . *thoughts*."

Matt glowed pink. "It . . . it does something to his hormones, you know? He may think you're something you're not."

"Something I'm not? Matt, you're talking in riddles."

Matt cleared his throat. "Kara, I don't like talking like this, but let me spell it out. Guys get turned on when they see a girl dressed in a . . . a sexy way. It sends them the wrong signals, the wrong messages. So, my brotherly advice to you is, keep the sweater on and don't do anything you might regret."

Kara fumed, pausing before shutting the door. "For goodness' sake, Matt. Just what do you take me for? How could I possibly get in trouble at Dee Ann's birthday party?"

Lord, it's so easy to make mistakes. The big ones are easier to avoid, but those little ones trip me. Before you know it, I'm sending others the wrong messages or ignoring who I am in You. Be the light to my path, and remind me to watch my modesty as well as my step. Thank You for caring about the little things as well as the big ones.

Additional Scripture reading: Matthew 6:25–34

❖

SMOKE OUT

Abstain from every form of evil.
—1 Thessalonians 5:22

Kara glided into a booth with Dee Ann and Brooke Kelly. Dee Ann pouted. "Kara, I thought you said Matt was driving you over."

"He had a date to study with a friend," Kara apologized. "But he'll be here to pick me up later."

Brooke giggled, brushing her silky waves of hair behind her back. She looked stunning in her shimmering turquoise jumpsuit accented with a thick gold chain. She gushed, "I didn't know Matt Daniels was your brother, Kara. He's cute, but he seems so serious."

Dee Ann added, "Serious, safe, and the best player on the Summitview High basketball team."

Kara nodded in agreement.

Brooke frowned and studied Dee Ann. "Safe from what?"

Dee Ann's blush glowed above her silky rose-colored blouse and suede jeans. "Well," she hesitated, "I bet he treats girls with respect."

Kara's heart skipped a beat when Todd James's smiling face leaned over the top of the booth. "Hmmm, he sounds boring to me."

The girls laughed. Todd scooted in the booth next to Brooke. Winking at Kara, he turned to Dee Ann. "Let me be the first to pay *my* respects. Happy Birthday!"

Dee Ann pulled a cigarette from her purse. "Men!"

"Do I detect a note of hostility in your voice?" Todd asked woundedly. His muscles rippled as he pulled off his leather jacket, revealing an aqua T-shirt that highlighted the depths of his eyes. "You don't have to turn sour just because you and Jack broke up."

Dee Ann's face burned with anger. "Who cares about Jack! Jack's a jerk! Guys like him seem to have only one thing on their minds."

"Which is?" Todd asked, feigning innocence.

Dee Ann lit her cigarette with shaking hands and inhaled deeply. The smoke curled around her words. "Oh, never mind. Kara knows what I mean."

Todd turned to Kara as Brooke reached for one of Dee Ann's cigarettes. "Really?" he asked. "Kara, maybe you could explain it to me."

Dee Ann's eyes blinked a warning as Kara flushed.

Before Kara could find her voice, the table server placed a bubbling pepperoni pizza before the hungry crowd. "Enjoy!" she said.

Kara caught her breath while the warm aroma encircled her friends. "Don't ask me, I just eat here," she quipped.

Todd chuckled. His attention made Kara feel giddy and a little frightened.

Could Todd be a shark, as Matt implied? Kara wondered. *What will I do if he asks me out?* She reached for a slice of pizza, warmed by a solution. *All I need is time, time to get to know Todd better.* Kara watched Dee Ann snuff out her cigarette. *At least Todd doesn't smoke, does he?*

As the meal progressed, Kara found herself caught in the excitement of the evening. She couldn't help noticing the sly smiles Todd continued to pass her way. *It feels good to belong to this group. They like me. I like them, too, especially Todd.*

With the last slice of pizza devoured, Dee Ann pulled out her cigarettes and offered them around. Kara's eyes widened. Todd reached for one and lit it, inhaling deeply.

He passed it to Kara. "You do smoke, don't you?"

Surprised at herself, Kara grasped the cigarette between her fingers, trying to look sophisticated. She hesitated then answered, "S-sure."

Dee Ann gave her a quizzical look as Kara's trembling hand flicked ash onto the table. *What do I think I'm doing?* Kara asked herself. She looked at the burning tobacco. *I can't actually smoke this thing, can I?* Todd's eyes encouraged her to take a puff. *Will I?*

When the air is thick with the smoke of the world, send Your Holy Spirit to breathe on me. When my thoughts are clouded with the wrong messages, help me switch to Your channel. I want to be in tune with You, regardless of the cost. Give me the power to avoid evil.

Additional Scripture reading: James 1:12–15

SMOKE SIGNALS

Beloved, do not imitate what is evil, but what
is good. He who does good is of God, but he
who does evil has not seen God.—3 John 1:11

Unable to take her eyes off Kara, Dee Ann fumbled with her package of cigarettes. Kara looked past the glowing embers, past her friend's unblinking eyes.

Now what do I do? I've either got to take a drag off this thing or put it out before it burns me.

"Nice weather we're having this fall," Kara blurted.

Dee Ann turned green. "Excuse me, Kara, I need a makeup check."

Glad to postpone the puff, Kara jumped up, balancing the burning cigarette between her fingers.

As Kara watched Dee Ann flee into the rest room, she failed to see the restaurant door open. Too late! Kara ducked into the booth.

She snuffed out the cigarette and shoved the ashtray to the far corner of the table.

Kara was surprised to note Todd looked delighted. *Why, Todd didn't want me to smoke the stupid thing,* she thought.

"Kara?" Matt snapped, eyeing the smoldering ashtray. "Are you ready to go home?"

Kara jumped. "Hi, Matt!"

She smoothed the sweater that still covered her bare shoulders and asked, "Aren't you early?"

Matt glared at the ashtray. "Obviously."

"I . . . I guess I'm ready, but first let me say good-bye to Dee Ann. She's in the rest room," Kara said.

Kara stumbled out of the booth, glad to delay facing Matt, although nervous about leaving him alone with Todd and Brooke.

When she reached the rest room, Kara found Dee Ann slouched over the sink. Kara gasped. "Dee Ann! Are you okay?"

"Yeah. My stomach feels a bit queasy. I must have eaten too much pizza." Dee Ann unhunched her shoulders and said, "I'm okay now."

"Good! Matt's here to pick me up, so I came to say good-bye."

"Matt?" Dee Ann questioned. "I wanted to say hi to him, but . . . you relay the message for me, okay?"

Kara arched a brow. *How could Dee Ann even think about guys after her date with Jack?* she wondered. "Sure, Dee Ann. See you tomorrow."

Why are my mistakes so often aired out for the world to see? It can be so embarrassing. I don't want to humiliate myself, and I don't want to humiliate You either. Help me to stand up for what I believe and live my life for You.

Additional Scripture reading: 1 Peter 1:13–21

❖

PEER POWER

A good name is to be chosen rather than great
riches.—Proverbs 22:1

Matt and Kara rode home in silence. When Kara spoke, her voice sounded small.

"Are you going to tell Mom and Dad?"

Matt bristled, steering around a corner. "Kara, I'm not your conscience. If anyone tells them about your new habit, *you* will have to do it."

"Matt, I know how it seemed. But I never inhaled, honest."

Flipping the blinker, Matt turned onto Mountain View Drive. "Kara, I can't tell you how to run your life. You have to make your own choices."

Kara folded her arms across her chest as the car slowed in front of their two-story home. "It's true I came close to making a mistake, but don't you see? I didn't. I didn't do anything wrong."

"Wrong?" Matt said. "Well, it seems to me you've already made several goofs."

"What do you mean?" Kara asked, her voice cracking with tension.

"For one thing, you discarded your best friend. Second, you joined a wild crowd, and now you've compromised your principles. What will your new friends think of you now? I'll tell you! They'll think you and your faith are a joke!"

"I told you I didn't smoke the stupid cigarette!"

"So you say," Matt said, pulling into the driveway. He turned and looked at his sister with disdain. "But if I hadn't walked in when I did, would you have taken a drag?"

Kara hung her head. "I'm not sure."

"That's what I meant earlier when I said hanging out with the wrong crowd is dangerous. The next thing you know, you're doing things you'd never dream of doing on your own." Matt turned off the engine and set the brake. "Tonight you got a little taste of the power others can have over you." He looked into Kara's eyes with a scowl. "I hope you learned your lesson."

Help me be a pillar of strength for my peers. If my friends are not the ones You'd have me hang out with, lead me to new ones. I give all my relationships to You. Help me overcome. Help me keep my name pure as I try to honor Yours.

Additional Scripture reading: 1 Thessalonians 4:9–12

❖

NOTE
OF DESPAIR

—

God is our refuge and strength,
A very present help in trouble.
—Psalm 46:1

The next morning, Kara rushed to leave the house. Her mother exclaimed, "Oh, I almost forgot. Jenni called while you were out last night."

"Ohmygosh!" Kara responded. She yelled to her brothers, already headed for the car, "Wait up! Jenni may need a ride."

She dialed the number. It rang—five times—six times—seven times. *She must have gone on,* Kara decided, hanging up.

But at school, there was no sign of Jenni at their usual hangout. Dee Ann wasn't around either, although Kara noticed Todd standing around with some guys. She waved, but he didn't appear to notice.

While I was in the rest room with Dee Ann, Matt probably preached him a sermon, Kara decided.

When the bell rang, Kara searched the hallway for Jenni's smile. It was missing. It was also missing from homeroom. First period, when Kara opened her algebra book, a note fluttered to the floor. It was written in Jenni's neat round lettering. It read,

Dear Kara,
I'm sorry for the trouble I've caused you the last few days. I can understand why you and your new friends don't want me hanging around. I'm just in the way. Give Matt a hug for me and tell him I'm sorry if I cause him any pain. But at least it won't be like he's losing a girlfriend.

*I'm sorry, but believe me, we'll all be better off. I enjoyed our
friendship while it lasted.*

Good-bye, Jenni

Kara read the note again. *Better off which way?* she pondered.
The note sounded so final . . . as if . . . OH, NO! Kara's heart froze
midbeat. *Jenni had seemed angry, but she wouldn't do anything to
harm herself, would she?*

Kara tried to look calm and raised her hand. Mr. Majors, the
math teacher, didn't like being disturbed mid-equation.

His voice clipped, "What is it, young lady?"

"Excuse me, but could I have a bathroom pass?"

She held her breath. The last person who had dared to ask such
a favor was publicly ridiculed.

"It's an emergency," she stuttered.

Mr. Majors peered over his bifocals. "Indeed," he said, scribbling Kara's escape note. "We don't want a puddle under your
desk."

The class snickered and Kara bolted for the door.

Once outside the room, Kara frowned. It was just her luck. A
teacher was standing guard on the other side of the girls' room.
How could she get around her? *Jesus, help me! Help Jenni!* she
pleaded, passing the guard.

"You there," the teacher spoke to Kara. "Let me see your pass."

Kara handed her the slip. "Hmmm, it says here you're on the
way to the bathroom. I think you missed your turn."

A cold chill ran through Kara. She had to get past this teacher
and on to Jenni before it was too late. *Stop Jenni from harming
herself!* she prayed. *Send Your angels!*

Kara answered, "I'm on my way to the office. I need to speak to
the principal."

"Hmmm. I'll make sure you get that interview. Follow me,
please."

*It's good I can call out to You in crisis situations. It's a privilege
I almost take for granted. But You are always there, and You al-*

ways hear my plea for help. Teach me to pray not only in emergencies but in every situation. Thank You for being there.

Additional Scripture reading: Hebrews 4:14–16

❖

DESPERATE ACT

The LORD is near to all who call upon Him,
To all who call upon Him in truth.
—Psalm 145:18

The teacher followed Kara into the principal's office. "I just caught Kara Daniels cutting class," she said.

Kara's heart beat like drums in concert. The school secretary pointed to a hard wooden chair. "Sit. Mr. Smith is busy. You'll have to wait."

Kara sat obediently, but her mind raced. She had to get out of there and fast!

Kara cleared her throat. "Excuse me, Ms. Parks?"

The secretary thumped her pen on her desk as if marking time she couldn't waste. "Yes?"

"I think my friend, Jenni Baker, is in trouble. I . . . I just found what appears to be a suicide note in my algebra book."

Ms. Parks's demeanor changed. "Jenni Baker? She's not in school today. I just called her house. No one was home."

The secretary rose, clicking her heels across the linoleum. She knocked on the principal's door, then stepped inside. Kara could hear muffled conversation.

Finally, Mr. Smith's voice rose. He said, "Bring her in."

Kara sat in front of the principal's desk while he finished jotting a note on a report. He looked up.

"What's all this about?" he asked.

Kara's hands shook as she shoved Jenni's letter toward him. "I found this in my algebra book. I think it's a suicide note."

Mr. Smith rubbed his bald head while he read.

Dear Jesus, this is taking too long, Kara complained in silent prayer.

"Has Jenni seemed upset or depressed lately?" Mr. Smith asked.

"Yes," Kara admitted. "We had a misunderstanding, a fight, I guess."

"I see," Mr. Smith responded, frowning. "Ms. Parks? Would you come in please?"

The secretary appeared at the door.

"Have you called Jenni's mother's work number?"

"Yes. But the line's busy."

Kara sank in her chair. *Are we running out of time?* The principal's phone rang. "Hello. Oh, yes, I can talk for a minute," he said. He looked up at Kara and motioned to the door. "Why don't you wait outside? I'm trying to deal with an urgent school board matter. I'll be back with you in a moment."

Kara stepped back into the outer office as the bell rang. Ms. Parks was nowhere in sight. Kara stood at the door, watching teenagers surge through the hall like schools of fish. She stepped into the flow, heading for the exit. Once there, she pushed the door open and ran. *Help me, Jesus,* she prayed. *Help me to get to Jenni in time.*

Sometimes, Lord, there seems to be no escape from the troubles of the world. No matter where I try to hide, trouble is hiding, too. But at the same time, You are with me. You are there, no matter how deeply into trouble I may go. Guide me and lead me to untroubled waters. Thank You for being near when I call to You.

Additional Scripture reading: Psalm 146:1–10

❖

THE DOORSTEP

Trust in the LORD with all your heart,
And lean not on your own
    understanding;
In all your ways acknowledge Him,
And He shall direct your paths.
    —Proverbs 3:5–6

Kara ran to the edge of the school property. When she reached the corner, she stopped, panting for breath. The traffic rolled through the intersection, ignoring her desperation to cross. Waiting for the traffic to clear, Kara prayed, *Lord, am I doing the right thing?*

In the recesses of her mind, Kara heard a quiet whisper, *Go back. Lord? Is that You?* Kara prayed.

The traffic continued its stream of chrome and exhaust. *Go back*, the voice spoke again.

Kara felt confused. Going back to Mr. Smith's office seemed illogical. He was too busy to help. But it would take Kara twenty or thirty minutes to run to Jenni's house. If Jenni had done anything to harm herself, it could be too late!

Kara turned around and looked at the school.

She hesitated. *Lord, I'm trusting You are speaking to me.*

Kara ran back into the building. When she entered the office door, Mr. Smith stepped beside her. "There you are. Shall we go?" he asked. "I just talked to Jenni's mom. She's going to meet us at their house."

Kara blinked with relief. Yet her voice was edged with concern as she asked, "Does Mrs. Baker know where Jenni is?"

"No, and she's worried," Mr. Smith replied. "She thought Jenni went to school today. Evidently, she didn't."

"Does she think Jenni stayed home sick?" Kara ventured.

"Perhaps, but Jenni doesn't answer the phone. We think something may be wrong. The Bakers are clear across town so they asked us to go on over and check out the situation. They'll get there as soon as they can."

The principal drove through the streets in silence while Kara watched houses blur together. How could she have been so callous toward Jenni? The events of the last few days seemed to have taken a life of their own. She hadn't meant to hurt Jenni, but . . .

The brakes squeaked, and Mr. Smith pulled his car in front of the Baker home. He and Kara stepped out of the car and approached the door. Knocking, Mr. Smith called, "Jenni, are you in there?"

A gust of wind blew a voiceless answer.

Mr. Smith rattled the doorknob.

"Jenni?" Kara called, her voice hoarse with emotion. Deep inside the house, Kara thought she heard a scraping sound. "Jenni, is that you?"

Lord, help me to listen for Your still, small voice. Sometimes I'm so distracted by the world, I forget to listen for You. Don't let me be confused by the Impostor, but help me tune my spirit to You so I can hear Your guiding voice as You direct my paths.

Additional Scripture reading: Psalm 16:7–11

FOUND!

Unless the LORD had given me help,
I would soon have dwelt in the silence
of death.—Psalm 94:17 (NIV)

Kara and Mr. Smith listened while the scraping sound grew louder. It was interrupted by a sharp bark.

Kara swallowed hard. "Jenni's dog, Nicki," she managed to squeak. "Ohmygosh! The rock!"

"Pardon?" Mr. Smith asked.

Kara was on her hands and knees. "The Bakers keep a key under one of these rocks in the flower bed!"

Leaping into the air, Kara held her prize above her head. "Here!" she shouted, racing for the door.

"Kara, wait!" Mr. Smith warned. "Don't open that door. Let me go first!"

Mr. Smith's warning came too late. Kara pushed and the door sprang open.

"Urfff!" Nicki squealed, his body sailing across the room.

"Oh! Sorry!" Kara apologized, flying into the house.

"Jenni? Are you here?" Kara called, scrambling from room to room. The principal followed, puffing behind her.

Kara ran up the stairs toward Jenni's room. "Jenni?"

Passing the closed bathroom door, Kara turned around. She knocked. "Jenni? Are you in there?"

There was no answer, except for a soft gurgling sound. Kara tried the knob. It was locked. She pounded again. "Jenni!"

Mr. Smith hurled his huge body at the door. The impact splintered it from the hinges. Mr. Smith tumbled inside with Nicki yapping at his heels

Swirls of dust from the newly cracked drywall circled Jenni's body. Kara stared in horror. Jenni lay in a crumpled heap, next to the bathtub. The room reeked with vomit. Jenni moaned and opened her eyes, and Mr. Smith knelt beside her.

He patted her cheeks with his hands. "Jenni, can you hear me?" he shouted. Jenni answered with a stream of vomit that coated Mr. Smith's trousers. "I'm dying," she moaned.

"Have you taken something?" Mr. Smith yelled.

Jenni nodded and closed her eyes.

Kara scanned the room, spotting an empty medicine bottle in the sink. She grabbed it. "Jenni, did you take this?"

Jenni nodded again, suppressing a gag. Tears of agony flowed down her face. "I thought it would stop the pain," she gasped.

Mr. Smith stood and turned to Kara. "I'm going to call 911. You stay here."

Kara knelt in a pool of vomit and hugged her friend. "Jesus, don't let her die!"

Life is precious, even when it's hard to face. Help me know You are by my side. You made me for a reason and a purpose. I am not a mistake. Keep me from the silence of death. Thank You for being there, and help me walk in Your love.

Additional Scripture reading: Psalm 27:13–14

VOICE
OF THE ENEMY

When I cry out to You,
Then my enemies will turn back;
This I know, because God is for
  me.—Psalm 56:9

The next morning, Kara returned to the hospital, still waiting for word on Jenni's condition. She blinked hard and wiped her eyes, pacing the hospital waiting room. *Why,* she wondered, *would Jenni want to kill herself?*

The past few days had been rough on Jenni, Kara knew. But this? Didn't Jenni know how much she was loved?

After what seemed like hours, Mrs. Baker came in and put her arm around Kara.

"Jenni's going to be okay," she said. "She's asking for you."

Kara peeked into Jenni's room to find Jenni draped in sheets that matched her pale complexion. Her blond curls were matted to her head. An intravenous tube dripped a clear liquid into one arm.

"Jenni," Kara said, sitting on the edge of the bed. "You okay?"

Jenni pulled her covers to her chin, trying to hide from Kara's concern. "Yeah, the doctor said I was just dehydrated."

Jenni searched the ceiling for some invisible pattern, and Kara reached for her hand. "I'm sorry, Jenni. I know I hurt you. You're going to be all right, aren't you?"

"I guess so."

Kara studied her friend.

Jenni blushed under Kara's probing eyes and turned her face to the wall. "Why?" she voiced for them both. "To tell you the truth, I'm not sure. All I know is I felt so alone, like my life was . . .

completely out of control." Jenni's eyes darted to Kara's. "That's when I heard a voice kind of coaching me to do what I did."

"A voice?"

"Don't tell anyone. I don't want everyone to think I'm crazy."

"So, what did this voice say?" Kara asked.

"It told me I was stupid and fat. It said I would be better off dead." Jenni bit her lip. "At first, I tried to push it away, but I couldn't. Finally, I began to believe it."

"That was the Enemy's voice!"

"The Enemy?"

"Of course!" Kara explained. "His voice is full of hate and lies. Satan knows how special you are to God and His kingdom. He knows God's got His mark on you and a special plan for your life."

Jenni's lip quivered. "I wish I could believe that."

"Jeff, the youth director at church, just talked about this," Kara explained. "He said some of our greatest Christian leaders have had suicidal thoughts at some point in their lives. He said we must constantly guard against the lies of the Enemy."

Jenni interrupted, "Do you really think I'm special?"

"There's no question about it," Kara answered, squeezing her friend's hand.

(To be prayed aloud.) *First, I rebuke all occultic activities in which I may have participated or occultic music to which I may have listened. Secondly, I pray:*

"Dear Heavenly Father, I know that You want the truth from me and that I must be honest with You. I have been fooled by Satan, the father of lies, and I have fooled myself. I thought I could hide from You, but You see everything and still love me. I pray in the name of the Lord Jesus Christ asking You to rebuke all of Satan's demons by Your power. I have asked Jesus into my life, and I am Your child. Therefore I command all evil spirits to leave me. I ask the Holy Spirit to lead me into all truth. I ask You to look right through me and know my heart. Show me if there is anything in me I am trying to hide, because I want to be free."—Quoted from Neil T. Anderson and Steve Russo, *The*

Seduction of Our Children (Eugene, Oregon: Harvest House, 1991) 221.

Additional Scripture reading: Psalm 42:1–6

IN
CHRIST
—

Reckon yourselves to be dead indeed to sin,
but alive to God in Christ Jesus our Lord.
—Romans 6:11

Kara looked down at her pale friend. "Are you feeling better?"

"Yes, but those pills really made me sick!"

"I know! You barfed all over Mr. Smith!"

Jenni's voice squeaked, "I did? How am I ever going to face him?"

"Don't worry. He'll get over it!" Kara said, laughing. "He was as glad to see you as I was." Kara caught Jenni's eyes. "Jenni, I have a question for you." Kara reddened. "I always assumed you were in Christ, but I've never made sure. Jenni, have you ever asked Christ into your life?"

"Yes," Jenni answered. "When I was eight. Our church was having a revival and I talked to a counselor. That night I prayed for Jesus to come into my heart and to forgive me."

"Do you realize," Kara asked, "how that changes your identity?"

Wrinkling her forehead, Jenni asked, "My identity?"

Kara picked up her denim purse and rummaged through it. "Yes, the Bible is clear that we have a new identity when we're in Christ."

"What do you mean?"

"Here are the notes I took from last Sunday's sermon. Let's see . . ." Kara read, "When we're in Christ, we're accepted and significant."

Jenni perched on one elbow. "Really?"

"Yes, and Romans 5:1 says we're justified and can have peace."

"What else does the Bible say?"

Kara squinted at her tiny lettering. "It says when we're in Christ, we're free from condemnation, can have Christ's mind, live in Christ, and Christ lives in us. We're also blessed, belong to God, possess the Holy Spirit, and uhhh . . ." Kara studied her list. "We've got God's grace. We've been seated with Christ and can approach God with freedom and confidence."

Kara's index finger continued to scan the column. "All of our debts have been canceled, and our old nature is removed. We're complete, made alive, and have the spirit of power, love, and self-discipline. We're saved and can find mercy and grace." Kara looked up. "Plus we're sanctified and have God's promises."

"Wow!" Jenni admitted, "I wish I'd known that before I swallowed those pills."

(To be prayed aloud.) *Lord Jesus, please come into my life, forgive me of my sins, and be my Lord.*

Thank You that Your Word says I am a new creature and a child of God. I am delivered from the power of darkness and transferred into God's kingdom. I am redeemed and blessed. I am strong and more than a conqueror. I am the light of the world and the salt of the earth. I am righteous and God lives in me. I have the power of the Holy Spirit, and this power is greater than the power of the Enemy, so I can do all things through Christ who strengthens me. As Your ambassador, I will tell the good news to others. But most of all, Lord, thank You that You will never leave me or forsake me.

Additional Scripture reading: Romans 6:20–23

❖

TEMPER TANTRUM

Cease from anger, and forsake wrath;
Do not fret—it only causes harm.
—Psalm 37:8

Later that afternoon, Kara meandered down the school hallway. She was lonesome without Jenni. Kara reflected on the events leading to the crisis. She thought, *This adventure's hardly started out the way I'd hoped.*

When Kara reached her locker, Rodger Tracey and his friends were waiting.

"Where's your fat friend?" Rodger asked with a sniff.

"Graduate or drop out!" Kara challenged.

"Ohhh, is it the wrong time of the month for you?" Rodger asked. He pinched Kara's arm. "That would explain why you look so fat."

Kara pushed Rodger and shouted, "You idiots! LEAVE ME ALONE!" Hallway greetings halted and Kara continued her tirade. "Don't you ever look at me, talk to me, or come near me again! Do you understand?"

Rodger laughed and stepped into Kara's space. As Kara backed away, she tripped over her purse and fell to the floor scattering her books.

"Sure, Miss High and Mighty. But you don't tell me what to do, understand?"

Matt stepped behind Rodger and tapped his shoulder. "That's my sister you're talking to. If you've got a problem with her, you'd better speak to me."

Rodger spun around, and his eyes flashed before traveling upward to peer into Matt's scowling face.

Rodger gulped and said, "You and Kara are related? My condolences."

The crowd continued to stare, circling closer, hoping for a fight. Rodger and his friends backed into the mob and disappeared into the hallway's hubbub.

Matt reached down for Kara's hand as the crowd dispersed. "Are you okay?"

"Yeah," Kara said, blushing.

"What's going on between you two?" Matt asked.

"Oh, Rodger made some rude remark about Jenni, and I lost my cool. He's been bugging me for a long time."

"Kara, I can understand how you feel, especially after yesterday, but you need to pull yourself together. Some people won't let you get away with moody behavior. They'll torment you just to see you blow."

Kara nodded. Dee Ann joined them with breathless excitement. "Kara, is everything all right?"

Shrugging, Kara said, "I guess so."

"Rodger is so crude," Dee Ann said. "Maybe you should report him to Mr. Smith."

Kara slugged her brother's arm. "There's no need for that when I've got Big Bro around."

"So, we finally meet!" Dee Ann said, turning to admire Kara's rescuer.

Matt's eyes twinkled. "You're Dee Ann Miller, aren't you?"

Smiling, Dee Ann said, "Yes, and I'm looking forward to knowing you better."

Guard my tongue and my temper, Lord, so they cause no harm. Help me not let my emotions get the best of me, but help me tame them. When I'm not feeling so great, remind me to use cool, pleasant words instead of hurtful, angry ones.

Additional Scripture reading: Colossians 3:12–17

❖

THE
BLUES

Fear not, for I am with you;
Be not dismayed, for I am your God.
I will strengthen you,
Yes, I will help you,
I will uphold you with My righteous
   right hand.—Isaiah 41:10

Saturday morning, Kara moped around the house, still reeling in the aftermath of the week's emotional storm. Shutting her bedroom door, she caught her grumpy reflection in the mirror. *Rodger's right,* she thought, pinching her waist. *I am pudgy.* Kara made a face at herself. *What's the matter with you? Is Stupid your middle name?*

She flopped on her bed, counting her failures. First of all, she'd betrayed Jenni. Second, she'd betrayed her standards by *almost* smoking a cigarette. Finally, she'd made a fool of herself with Rodger.

Kara rolled over and stared at the ceiling. *What's the old baseball saying? Three strikes and you're out?*

Well, she pondered, *it might be true I have the mind of Christ, but it's also true I don't always use it. In fact, it's quite possible I may have even lost it.*

Kara furrowed her eyebrows. *What's that passage in Romans? Oh, yeah.* She recited it from memory: "There is therefore now no condemnation to those who are in Christ Jesus. Romans 8:1."

Kara stared at the iris border that made her white ceiling look like the lid to a lavender box. *Is it possible that passage is true? If we love and follow Jesus, does He really look the other way when it comes to our mistakes?*

Blushing, Kara thought of her recent blunders. *I'm really sorry for all my goofs, Lord,* she prayed. *Thank You for not condemning me but forgiving me.*

She sat up. *But, Lord, I'll make it up to You. I'll do my best to get my life back into shape. I'll do it right this time.*

Lord, it's easy to get confused about my life. So often I do the wrong thing, even when I have the right thing in mind. When I do, I get really down on myself and wonder why I can't do better. Thank You for understanding and always giving me another chance. But while I struggle, help me not to take back the control of my life or try to do things in my own strength. Help me continue to submit to You.

Additional Scripture reading: Isaiah 43:18–21

❖

SORTING IT OUT

Flee also youthful lusts; but pursue
righteousness, faith, love, peace with those
who call on the Lord out of a pure heart.
—2 Timothy 2:22

"Kara," Mrs. Daniels called from below, "I need your help." Kara let her feet thud down the stairs.

Her mom looked up. "Goodness, I thought you were a herd of elephants."

"Must be the extra weight I've gained," Kara spouted.

"You look great!" Mrs. Daniels complimented, pulling baby clothes from a dusty box.

"What are you doing?" Kara asked.

"I thought I'd sort through some of these old things. The Summitview Crisis Pregnancy Center is desperate for baby clothes."

"But these are our memories, our childhoods," Kara lamented, clutching a tiny pink dress.

"It's hard for me, too," her mom admitted. "Every time I pick up an outfit, memories of my three babies flood me," she said, caressing a tiny suit. "Do you remember how cute Bryce looked in this? He wore it on his first birthday."

"I do remember," Kara said. "That's why I don't understand. Why would you want to give these things away?"

Mrs. Daniels sighed. "There was an item in our church bulletin that said the Crisis Pregnancy Center is desperate for baby clothes. It doesn't seem right to hoard these so I thought I'd sort through a few and send some over."

"What's the Crisis Pregnancy Center?" Kara asked.

Mrs. Daniels's eyes embraced a pink jumpsuit before she folded it into a box. "The center helps women who have unplanned or crisis pregnancies. Staff members even counsel women who have experienced the trauma of an abortion."

Kara felt her selfishness melt into curiosity. "Do they have pregnancy testing?"

"It's free and confidential," Mrs. Daniels said. "They even offer moms-to-be counseling, maternity and baby clothes, baby furniture, and housing."

Kara folded a piece of her childhood, and tucked it into the carton. "I wonder who will end up with these clothes?"

Mrs. Daniels's eyebrows arched. "You might be surprised, Kara. It could even be someone from your high school. The center counsels a lot of teenagers."

"I know a lot of the girls are sexually active. I've seen them in the bathroom, popping their birth control pills."

"It's really sad to see those girls give away something so intimate. Sex is like a beautiful gift, wrapped in silver paper. When we tear off the wrappings and share the treasure with another person, we give away a part of ourselves. If or when another partner comes along, he'll find the beauty of the gift tarnished, missing some of its essence.

"If this gift is shared with many more partners, the treasure will be broken and its beauty lost. The gift will lose its intimacy, and the giver will lose her feelings of self-worth."

"Mom, what if a girl's already wasted her gift? Is there anything she can do to regain it?" Kara asked.

"God can restore her esteem with His unconditional love, but her regrets and broken dreams will always be a part of her life. Yet, she can choose to end her destructive cycle. She can stop spending her treasure and save what's left as a gift for her future husband," Mrs. Daniels said.

She reached for Kara's hand. "Be careful. Your gift is too priceless and fragile to waste."

The world sends such strong lies about the value of our sexuality and personhood, I sometimes feel confused. Help me see sex is not a recreational activity or something I should do to gain a boyfriend. Help me be strong enough to say no, even if I lose my chance to date the guy of my dreams.

Even in the pain of possible rejection, I know You will honor my decision. In the end, I will gain much more than I could ever lose.

Additional Scripture reading: Romans 12:1–2

ANSWERING THE CALL

Great peace have those who love
   Your law,
And nothing causes them to
   stumble.—Psalm 119:165

Kara laid a sleeper into the box and imagined the baby soon to wear it. The baby's image shattered with the ringing of the phone.

"I got it!" Bryce yelled from the kitchen. "Kara, it's for you. It's a boyyy!"

Kara's heart leapt. *A guy? Who would be calling me?* Grabbing the phone, she rushed Bryce out of the room.

"Hello?"

"Kara! I haven't seen you since Dee Ann's birthday party. I called to see how you're doing."

"Todd?" Kara said with a gulp. She hadn't prepared herself for a phone call from him. "Fine! Uh, how have you been?"

"Great! I was just promoted to team captain, and I thought maybe you and I could go out and celebrate."

Kara's mind flashed an alarm. She liked Todd, but she hardly knew him. "You mean alone?"

"Of course!" Todd chuckled. "Unless you want your brother to come along." He laughed. "By the way, Matt looked a little bent out of shape when he picked you up the other night. Is everything okay?"

"Yeah, Matt can be a little stuffy sometimes," Kara confided.

"He can't be too stuffy. I heard he and Dee Ann are going out tonight."

Kara blinked surprise. It wasn't like Matt to miss a church youth group meeting. "You're kidding!"

"Dee Ann says he's picking her up at seven."

"Matt and Dee Ann! Who would have thought?" Kara exclaimed.

"Dee Ann for one. She seems pretty excited."

An ugly thought crept into Kara's mind: *Was that the reason Dee Ann befriended me this past week?* Kara pushed the idea away.

"You didn't answer my question," Todd reminded her. "How about you and me grabbing a bite to eat tonight?"

"I guess so. Sure," Kara said, still thinking about Matt and Dee Ann. After all, Matt couldn't give her a hard time about her new friends if he was dating one of them, could he?

"Seven o'clock?"

"That would be great," Kara answered, feeling a butterfly flutter in her stomach.

She hung up. *Is it safe to go out with someone I hardly know?*

She hoped so. *Keep me safe tonight, and help me get to know Todd better,* she prayed.

Dating is intimidating, Lord! Help me find creative solutions to allow me to develop special friendships with guys without temptation. I want to honor You with my body and avoid situations that would cause me to stumble. Help me to sense Your presence everywhere I go.

Additional Scripture reading: Psalm 51:10–13

GETTING READY

Know also that wisdom is sweet to your
   soul;
if you find it, there is a future hope for you,
and your hope will not be cut off.
   —Proverbs 24:14 (NIV)

Kara swirled a hot curling iron through her hair, trying to control her trembling hands. *I never even imagined that Todd would notice me, much less ask me out,* she thought with a smile. *He's the most gorgeous guy in school!*

She patted blush on her cheeks and stepped back, studying her image in the mirror.

Her ruby jeans complemented her white ruffled blouse and tapestry vest swathed with roses. She tilted her head. *What's missing?* Rummaging through her jewelry box, she pulled out a gold heart that dangled from a long chain and slipped it around her neck. She smiled at her reflection, watching her brown curls float around her face. The necklace was exactly what her outfit needed.

Bouncing down the stairs, she saw Matt pick up the keys and push his wallet into his pocket. He looked nice in his cords and indigo sweater.

"There you are. Are you ready?" he asked.

"Ready?" Kara asked, confused. "I thought you had a big date tonight."

Matt grinned sheepishly. "I hope you don't mind. I asked Dee Ann to come with us to youth group."

Kara froze on the bottom step. "Youth group? She said yes to that?"

"Well, I know it's not like a real date. But it will give us a chance to get to know each other better. Are you ready?"

"Yes . . . I mean . . . no," Kara said with a frown. "I have other plans tonight."

"You and Jenni finally getting back together?" Matt asked. "I don't think Dee Ann would mind if the two of you joined us."

Lowering her voice, Kara said, "Maybe, but Jenni would."

"What?"

"Matt, I've got a date tonight."

"With who?"

"Todd."

"Oh," Matt said, scowling. "I thought I warned you about him."

"Give me a break, Matt," Kara exclaimed. "I think Todd seems like a nice guy. I just want a chance to get to know him better. That's all."

The doorbell rang and Matt opened the door.

"Hi, Todd," he said, grabbing Todd's hand. "I hear you're going out with Kara tonight."

Todd grinned into Matt's glare.

"Take good care of Kara, you hear?"

"Sure, Matt," Todd said, pulling his hand away and flexing his fingers. "I'll be a perfect gentleman."

When Matt left, Todd asked Kara, "Is he always so serious?"

Kara smiled an apology. "Sorry, Todd, it's just that Matt's a little protective."

"Oh," Todd said, rubbing his hand. "Well, shall we go?"

"First, I'd like you to meet my parents."

"Sure," Todd said as Kara guided him to the den. Kara said a quick prayer: *Make this evening turn out all right, Lord. Please!*

It's so exciting to experience some aspects of this life. But help me never be blinded by the rush of activities that sometimes swallows me. May I listen to You and seek Your wisdom so I'll make the right choices. May I stay strong in You.

Additional Scripture reading: James 1:2–8

❖

NIGHT OF ROMANCE?

No temptation has overtaken you except such as is common to man; but God is faithful, who will not allow you to be tempted beyond what you are able, but with the temptation will also make the way of escape, that you may be able to bear it.—1 Corinthians 10:13

Kara fidgeted with her gold heart as Todd drove them into the night. *Here I am with the guy of my dreams, and I'm too dumb to think of anything to say,* she scolded herself.

Todd flashed her a smile and patted her knee.

Kara smiled back, noticing how great Todd looked in his denim shirt and jeans. She blushed under his gaze. "So, where are you taking me?"

"There's a little cafe just above Boulder I thought you'd like."

"Boulder? That's so far!"

"Only thirty minutes if you drive like I do."

Todd laughed as Kara rechecked her seat belt. "Don't worry, Kara. I haven't lost anyone yet."

"Thanks for the consolation," Kara said, trying to smile. "How long did you say you've been driving?"

"Over a year! I'm certified safe!" Todd raced through a yellow light. "See, no problem!"

As they started up the canyon, Kara pushed her foot to the floorboard as if trying to slow Todd's speed. Todd grinned, agitating her concern by hugging his car along the curves of the mountain road.

"Where's this cafe?" Kara asked, hoping they'd arrive soon.

"First, a little detour," Todd said, slowing down. "There, a perfect spot." He pulled onto a turnaround that overlooked the city of Boulder. The city lights winked while Todd pushed up the steering wheel and reclined his bucket seat. He smiled. "Why don't you come over and join me?" he asked.

Kara froze while Todd unsnapped her seat belt and reached for her hand. "Come on. Don't be bashful."

Pulling her hand away, Kara said, "I can't, Todd. I hardly know you."

"Here's your chance to know me better," Todd said, lacing his fingers through hers. He pulled Kara to him, kissing her lips.

Shaken from the hunger of his touch, Kara pushed herself away. "No, Todd. This isn't right."

Todd drew her back, holding her tight in his powerful arms. Kara could feel herself melt into the warmth of his body.

"No!" she gasped. "This isn't what I want!" He let her slip through his arms as she grabbed the door handle and stumbled into the night air, snapping the chain of her necklace on the turn signal. The gold heart and chain fell in a heap on the floorboard.

Todd picked them up and followed. "Kara? I thought you liked me."

Kara whirled to face him, her voice breathless from the power of their embrace. "I do, I think," she said. "But, Todd, I've just met you. Don't rush me like this."

"Kara, when you like someone, you show it. A little affection never hurt anyone." Todd stretched his arms toward her. "Come on, Kara, let's get back into the car."

"I'd like to go home."

"What? I don't understand."

Tears stung Kara's eyes. "I think we have a different set of values, Todd. I don't think this is going to work."

"Values . . . as in what?"

"I've made a commitment to myself," Kara explained, "to keep myself pure for the man I'll marry."

"I don't want to make love to you, Kara," Todd scolded. "I just want to fool around a little. What's wrong with that?"

Kara gulped, looking into Todd's earnest eyes. The intensity of his gaze made her pulse race. How could she explain?

Lord, when situations get too hot to handle, help me find a way of escape—even when escaping seems to be the last thing I really want to do. Remind me of my commitments, and help me to find the words and actions I need so I can handle any temptations that come my way.

Additional Scripture reading: 1 Corinthians 10:10–20

NIGHT FLIGHT

It is God's will that you should be holy; that you should avoid sexual immorality. . . . For God did not call us to be impure, but to live a holy life.—1 Thessalonians 4:3, 7 (NIV)

An explanation would be useless, Kara thought, turning her back to Todd. *He just wouldn't get it.*

Kara began walking down the dark canyon road toward the lights of Boulder.

"Hey, where are you going?" Todd called. "You can't walk home from here. It's too dangerous."

Hugging her arms across her chest, Kara pressed on. "Less dangerous than getting back into the car with you," she shot back.

"Wait," Todd called, catching her stride. "Stop and talk to me."

Kara stopped. "All right."

"What is it with you? No other girl's ever walked out on me mid-kiss."

"Todd, we hardly know each other. Do you realize this is our first real conversation? You're moving fast, too fast."

"I'm sorry, Kara. Maybe I got carried away. You really excite me, you know?"

"That's just it," Kara explained. "You excite me, too."

"So, what's the problem?"

"The problem is, I don't want a relationship built on lust. I want to know what you're about. I want you to know what I'm about."

"You mean you want to talk?" Todd looked as if he finally understood and pressed Kara's gold heart and broken chain into her hand. "I can do that. We'll kiss later."

"That's not what I mean."

Todd released Kara's hand from his. "You don't like kissing?"

"I do," Kara confessed, slipping the gold heart into her vest pocket. "I couldn't handle reclining with you like that. It was too intimate." Kara forced a laugh. "I never recline on dates."

Todd's eyebrows arched. He asked, "What's wrong with reclining?"

"It's too compromising. Things could get out of control."

Todd was quiet. "Come back to the car with me, Kara. I promise I'll be a gentleman. We'll talk, okay?"

Kara breathed a sigh of relief. "Okay, but would you mind if we went back to town? This place is too romantic. I don't know if I can trust you here."

Todd grinned. "Sure, Kara, whatever you say."

Thank You that You always provide a way out of whatever temptation I may face. Sometimes the way is clouded by my longing to flirt with danger, but it's there. Remind me to stay holy by sticking close to You.

Additional Scripture reading: 1 John 2:15–17

MAGIC
AT McGUFFY'S

Let him know that he who turns a sinner from
the error of his way will save a soul from
death and cover a multitude of sins.—James
5:20

Todd pulled into a parking space at McGuffy's, and he and Kara
went inside. When they got their order, they found a secluded table
in the play yard.

The evening breeze rippled Todd's hair, and the full moon peeked
from behind a stray cloud. "Kara, you really intrigue me. What
makes you so different from the other girls?"

"I guess you could say that I don't live for the moment," Kara
said in the soft glow of the moonlight. "I've thought through a lot
of issues. I've made choices. Some of my choices are hard . . . like
snuffing out that cigarette the other night. But I don't want bad
decisions to keep me from finding my dreams."

"Dreams? What do you dream about?"

"I'd like to study journalism. Eventually, I'd like to marry and
have a family."

"Lofty goals," Todd admitted.

"What are your dreams, Todd?"

Todd opened his hamburger and squeezed a packet of ketchup
onto his steaming double-beef patty. "I don't know. I guess I'm
hoping for a football scholarship and maybe a degree in business."

"Business?" Kara asked. "What kind of business are you interested in?"

"Well, my dad owns a print shop. I'll probably go into business
with him someday."

Todd studied Kara intently. "So, your decision to avoid kissing me is one of the choices you've made?"

Kara managed to swallow a sip of her shake before bursting into laughter. "No, I never said I wanted to avoid kissing altogether. It's just that a guy has to earn the right to kiss me."

"You mean, if a guy spends a little money on you, it would be okay to smooch a little?"

"No!" Kara exclaimed, smiling shyly. "My kisses aren't for sale. What I meant to say is . . . I need to have a deep friendship with a guy before we . . . uh . . . kiss. And even then, the kisses should take place in a safe place. Like at my doorstep." She cleared her throat nervously. "Reclining in romantic out-of-the-way places is . . . out."

"Isn't that a little old-fashioned, Kara?"

"Maybe. But it's what I want."

"I guess I'm surprised that you would have this all figured out. What makes you come up with these ideas?"

"It's my faith."

"Faith in what, yourself?"

"No, it's my faith in my Lord, Jesus Christ."

Todd almost dropped his hamburger. "You mean you're a Jesus freak?"

"I don't consider myself a freak, but I do love Jesus," Kara responded. "What do you know about Him, Todd?"

"Not much, I guess."

Kara ventured to ask, "Would you like to know more?"

It's great how You can turn a bad situation into an opportunity. Give me boldness to share my faith in You. So many people have never even considered what You have to offer them. Help me give them a reason to look in Your direction. Show me how to help others cover their sins.

Additional Scripture reading: 1 John 5:4–12

❖

JESUS
WHO?

**For God so loved the world that He gave His
only begotten Son, that whoever believes in
Him should not perish but have everlasting
life.—John 3:16**

Todd's scowl was hidden as the moon darted behind a cloud.
"Are you a member of some kind of cult?"

Kara suppressed a chuckle and reached for a fallen pickle. "I
get my beliefs from the Bible."

"The Bible? I've never read it. What's it about?"

"Basically, it's a love letter from God to us. It's full of stories
about how God loves and forgives us."

Todd took a slow sip of his shake. "Which of these stories is most
important?"

Dipping a fry into her ketchup, Kara stared into the darkness. "I
guess the story of Jesus. His life echoes God's message of love."

"How?"

Kara reached for a napkin and explained, "You see, people got
lost from God because of their mistakes or sins. So, God allowed
people to sacrifice animals to hide their sins so that their relationship
might be restored. But the animal sacrifices were never-ending because people kept blowing it with more sins."

"So, how does this Jesus guy fit in?" Todd asked, reaching for
a fry.

"Jesus is God's Son, sent to this earth and born to a virgin. Jesus
was totally innocent.

"When Jesus died on the cross, He became our once-and-for-all
sacrifice. Because He was pure, His blood worked as payment for

your sins, my sins, and everyone's sins. Jesus rose from the dead by God's power. Now, He is with God, the Father.

"Because of what Jesus did, God can hear us. God can be our Lord, King, and Friend."

"That's some story, Kara. It's funny I've never heard it before. So you say we're all forgiven and can talk with God?"

"Yes, if we recognize Jesus as God's Son and ask Him to forgive us."

Kara studied Todd's almost-eager eyes. "Would you like to ask Jesus to forgive you and to take over your life?"

Rubbing his salty hands together, Todd said, "It sounds interesting, but I'd have to say no. I enjoy my life the way it is. The last thing I need is more rules to follow."

"This isn't a game of rules," Kara explained. "It's an adventure. When Jesus is a part of your life, you do good because you want to please Him."

Todd watched the traffic rumble down Main street. "Maybe later," he finally said. "I don't need any complications in my life just now."

Help me know the why and what of what I believe. Help me have an answer for anyone who should happen to ask me about my faith. I've taken so much of Your love for granted, I haven't realized how great it is. Reveal Your truth to me and teach me Your ways.

Additional Scripture reading: 1 Peter 3:13–16

MESSAGE
TO FORGIVE

Then Peter came to Him and said, "Lord, how often shall my brother sin against me, and I forgive him? Up to seven times?" Jesus said to him, "I do not say to you, up to seven times, but up to seventy times seven."—Matthew 18:21–22

Horns honked and headlights shone on Kara and Todd as they sat in their outdoor hideaway. They blinked against the brightness of the beams.

Todd squinted. "Friends of yours?"

Kara shielded her eyes and studied the silhouettes of teenagers who were tumbling from the cars.

"Oh, the youth group must have let out early. That's Matt and his friends."

"Youth group?"

"Yeah, we meet whatever Friday or Saturday nights don't conflict with Summitview High's football games."

"What do you guys do there?"

"We study the Bible, play games, and talk a lot. It's fun!"

Matt and Dee Ann burst through the gate surrounding the fenced play area, holding hands. "Hi, guys!" Matt called. "Do you mind if we join you?"

"Go ahead," Todd answered.

Matt and Dee Ann sat down. "Nice night to be outside," Matt commented. He noticed Kara's broken chain dangling from her pocket. "What happened to your necklace?"

Kara flushed. Matt would have to notice. She tried to sound nonchalant. "Oh, I caught it on the door when I got out of the car."

Matt glared at Todd. "Oh?"

Laughing teenagers scattered through the picnic area with food and drinks, and Kara asked, "What did Jeff talk about tonight?"

"He led a Bible study on forgiveness," Matt answered.

Kara turned to Dee Ann. "Did you enjoy it?"

"I did," Dee Ann admitted.

Matt observed, "Jeff said we need to forgive everyone."

Looking down at the table, Dee Ann said, "I don't know if I'm ready for that. That would seem too much like encouraging some people to hurt me."

"I disagree," Matt commented. "Yeah, we're supposed to forgive others, but that doesn't mean we have to continue to let them push us around. We have the right, perhaps even an obligation, to stand up for ourselves as well as our beliefs."

"I don't know much about the Bible," Todd confessed, "but I have heard it says you're supposed to turn the other cheek."

"True," Matt agreed. "But that doesn't mean we have to *stay* in abusive situations. Sometimes we need to forgive at a distance."

Dee Ann nodded. "That's an interesting thought, Matt."

The thought of forgiving some people seems nearly impossible. But even so, I know that's what You want me to do. Teach me how to give my hurts to You and let You shine Your forgiving love through me. When life isn't fair, help me learn to go on and not fall into the trap of bitterness.

Additional Scripture reading: Matthew 18:23–35

FORGIVE THAT?

For if you forgive men their trespasses, your
heavenly Father will also forgive you. But if
you do not forgive men their trespasses,
neither will your Father forgive your
trespasses.—Matthew 6:14–15

The door of the restaurant flew open, and an intoxicated Jack
Raymond swaggered out. Balancing a tray laden with food, he
scanned the crowd.

Spotting Dee Ann, he said, "Well, if it isn't my little slut." The
noisy mob hushed.

Dee Ann tried to shrink into her seat. Kara reached for Dee
Ann's hand. "Ignore him, Dee. He's drunk."

Jack barreled his hulk toward their table, and Matt vaulted to his
feet. "Jack, you're not welcome here. Why don't you go inside?"

Jack studied Dee Ann hungrily, then snarled at Matt, "Well,
Church Boy, what are you doing hanging out with this trash? Aren't
you afraid she'll ruin your reputation?"

Dee Ann stumbled from her bench, backing away. "Go away,
Jack. You're mean when you're drunk."

"You should know, Babe. You seem to like it," Jack said, continu-
ing his advance.

As Dee Ann cowered behind Matt, Matt warned, "Jack, stay
away!"

Todd, who was watching Jack from his seat, turned to Kara.
He whispered, "Explain it again. Why do you believe in forgiving
others?"

Kara shook her head, too stunned to speak.

Todd rose to his feet. "Kara, it's been fun," he said. "I'll call you later. Right now I've got to get this big oaf home before he hurts someone." He stepped toward Jack and called his name.

Teetering, Jack tried to focus. "Todd, is that you?" he asked.

Todd said, "Yes, and you're just the man I wanted to see." He maneuvered to Jack's side. "This place is too-crowded. Let's go for a little ride." Grabbing Jack's arm and his food, Todd managed to turn him toward the gate.

Jack's face broke into a grin. He slurred, "Sure, Todd, it's a little stuffy out here anyway."

Todd herded Jack into his car and waved good-bye.

Dee Ann collapsed onto the bench.

"See what I mean, Kara?" Dee Ann whispered. "Would Jesus expect me to forgive something like that?"

Matt sat down next to her. "So what's this between you and Jack?" he asked.

Dee Ann bit her lip. "He's just mad because I won't go out with him. That's all."

When You say I should forgive others, do You mean everyone? Some people are so unlovable and cruel. But because You asked, I'm willing to try. Show me how and give me opportunities to love the unlovable. But while I'm trying, keep me safe in Your love.

Additional Scripture reading: Luke 6:37–42

DIET
BENT

God shows personal favoritism to no man.
—Galatians 2:6

Monday morning, Kara found Jenni hiding in the shadows of the school steps, prepping for a history test.

"There you are," Kara called, eyeing Jenni's text. "I hope I'm not interrupting the battle of Waterloo or anything. Why didn't you answer your phone this morning?"

Jenni snapped her book shut. "Mom drove me over earlier. I didn't want to bother you."

"Bother me?" Kara exploded, "Are you kidding? You're my best friend."

Jenni watched Todd wave in Kara's direction. "Yeah, but you don't need me anymore. You've got other friends."

Jenni watched Todd stride toward them. "Todd looks much more exciting than I do."

Kara returned Todd's wave, then faced Jenni. "I could never have a better friend than you, Jenni. I'm not planning to turn my back on you, now or ever."

Todd joined the twosome. "Hi, Kara. Who's your friend?"

Putting her arm around Jenni, Kara said, "I'm glad you asked. This happens to be Jenni Baker, my best friend in the whole world."

Jenni flushed under Todd's gaze. "Nice to meet you," Todd smiled a hello before turning to Kara. "I'm sorry I didn't get back with you Saturday night. But I had to get Jack sobered up before I could deliver him to his doorstep."

Jenni's mouth fell open, and her eyes bounced from Kara to Todd.

"I wanted to thank you for saving Matt from a fight," Kara replied.

"Besides, Dee Ann was pretty shook up. I spent the rest of the evening trying to console her."

Waving at one of his friends, Todd said, "Gotta go. I'll call you later, all right?"

"Yeah. That'll be great."

Jenni's eyes were bright with question marks. "What's the story? You, Matt, Jack, and Todd went drinking with Dee Ann?"

Kara defended herself. "Of course not. Todd and I were at McGuffy's . . ."

"You and Todd?"

"Yeah, when Matt and Dee Ann showed up."

Jenni's shoulders slumped.

"I'm sorry, Jenni. Matt took Dee Ann to youth group with him. He was thinking about inviting you, too."

Jenni shook her head. "Matt's not interested in me. Why should he be when he can go out with beautiful cheerleaders like Dee Ann?"

"But you're beautiful, too," Kara said. "Besides, you'll never guess who Matt said was asking for you."

"Who?"

"Ryan Stephens!"

Jenni wrinkled her nose. "Oh. He always bugs me."

"What?" Kara asked, stepping back to stare at her friend. "Why haven't you told me?"

"I was going to. But it's just . . ."

Kara giggled. "Just what?"

"He's so thin," Jenni whispered.

"So? Do you judge a guy by his weight?"

Jenni looked ashamed. "Pretty two-faced of me, don't you think? Look at me. I need to lose fifteen pounds!"

Thumping her almost-flat stomach, Kara said, "I've been thinking about getting into shape myself."

"You? You're as skinny as a twig!"

"Why don't we go on a diet together? We'll jog home from school and cut our fat intake. What do you say?"

"Sure," Jenni agreed. "It would be fun to have a partner. Besides, I'm ready to try anything."

Since my body is Your temple, help me to eat the right foods and get plenty of sleep and exercise. Lord, I give any bad habits that might harm my body to You. Teach me moderation with junk food, and help me to totally avoid drugs, alcohol, and tobacco.

Additional Scripture reading: 2 Peter 1:1–9

❖

BIG BUSINESS

You shall not murder.—Exodus 20:13

Kara's heart pounded in rhythm with her feet as the wind pushed against her body. Jenni's laughter rang in her ears as the twosome raced to Kara's front porch.

"I won!" Kara cheered, slinging her body into the wooden swing a breath before Jenni. The impact of the landings caused quivers to ride up the swing's chains to the ceiling.

Kara pushed off with her feet, and the twosome rocked into laughter.

"We've got to race every day," Kara said. "If we do, our waists will trim down in no time."

Jenni nodded in agreement, too tired to speak.

"Kara?" Mrs. Daniels called from inside the house. "Would you and Jenni come here? There's someone I want you to meet."

Kara and Jenni exchanged glances before abandoning their rest.

"Help yourself to a glass of milk and cookies first," Mrs. Daniels called.

Jenni ogled the chocolate chip cookies, begging Kara with her eyes. "No, Jenni," Kara said, "we must not bend to the pressure of chocolate."

The girls poked their heads into the living room. Kara said, "Hi, Mom."

She studied a young blond dressed in a denim skirt and peach camp shirt sitting next to her mother.

Mrs. Daniels said, "Kara, this is my friend, Sara Penrose. She's telling me about a prayer vigil planned for the Summitview Women's Clinic a few weeks from now."

As Kara and Jenni sat down, Jenni asked, "Prayer vigil? You're planning one of those violent abortion protests like I've seen on TV?"

Sara laughed. "You can't believe everything you see in the media. Besides, violence is the last thing we have in mind. Our group meets outside the clinic the first Saturday of every month. We stand on the sidewalk and pray."

Kara cocked her head. "What do you pray about?"

"Mainly for the girls and women inside and for their unborn babies," Sara answered.

Jenni said, "Babies? I thought abortions took place only when the fetuses were a clump of cells."

"We're all clumps of cells! The word *fetus* is a dehumanized term to describe a *baby*," Sara said. "A *baby* develops rapidly in the womb. After only thirteen days, every part of the baby's body has already begun to form. By the eighteenth day, the baby's heart is beating, and by the forty-second day, the baby's brain is active. In the seventh or eighth week, a time when many children are aborted, the baby has fingerprints and can feel pain."

"You're kidding!" Jenni exclaimed. "I never knew that! If fetuses are babies, why do people abort them?"

"Mainly because abortion is big business," Sara explained. "A business that has successfully marketed the 'choice' concept to unsuspecting women. Some clinics will do anything to get patients. One former clinic owner recently admitted to generating potential clients by speaking to groups of young girls about safe sex. Then when some of the girls came to her for birth control pills, she deliberately prescribed improper dosages, hoping to get their business later."

Sara continued, "It's unbelievable that this industry can get away with murder. Our prayer vigil prays that people will recognize the killings as well as the unethical practices of the industry."

Kara's mom agreed. "That's why I'm going to the prayer vigil. Maybe you girls would like to come along. We hope to even counsel some of the girls who may be on their way to abort their babies."

"I'll think about it," Kara answered. "I don't know how I'd feel if someone from school went inside. It would be, you know, too strange."

Sara said, "If you decide to come, you'll be at risk for recognizing some of your schoolmates. But because they know you, your presence could make the difference between life and death for their babies. Let me know what you decide to do. It could turn out to be quite an adventure."

Help me appreciate and respect the life that You create. I pray for the pregnant girls at my school, that they will not destroy the lives of their unborn. Take the blinders off and expose the truth that abortion is murder.

Additional Scripture reading: Psalm 139:13–16

BIG
LETDOWN

Do not be unequally yoked together
with unbelievers. For what fellowship has
righteousness with lawlessness? And what
communion has light with darkness?
—2 Corinthians 6:14

Kara had just slid her favorite vintage musical into the video player and pressed "play" when the phone rang. Her mother groaned, "There it goes again. Every time we try to have a little family fun, we're interrupted by the phone."

Bryce was already on his feet, toppling his bowl of popcorn onto the carpet. "I'll get it!"

Kara winced as he called, "Kara, it's for you. It's that boyyy again!"

Pushing Bryce back into the strains of musical dialogue, Kara shut the door, muffling a heart-wrenching love song. "Hello? Todd?"

"Hi. I called to see how you're doing."

Kara leaned against the wall as if to steady herself. Taking a deep breath, she answered, "Fine. How about you?"

"Great! Listen, the Homecoming dance is coming up. I was calling to see if you'd like to go."

Kara's heart skipped a beat. "I'd love to, but . . ."

"But what?" Todd asked.

"I like you. I like you a lot," Kara answered. "But we're so different. Maybe we shouldn't go out anymore."

"Haven't you heard? Variety is the spice of life," Todd challenged. "So, we're different. But I'm fascinated by you. I know we'd have a great time."

Turning to the wall, Kara hung her head. "I'd like to go, Todd.

But I'm not sure if you respect my faith enough. That part of me is too important to push into the background."

"Kara, I didn't ask to marry you," Todd snorted. "I just asked to take you to the dance. What's the big deal?"

"It's just that it's important to me that my guy appreciates what I believe. I want to be able to talk the same language and maybe even pray together."

"It sounds like you're looking for a groom, not a date," Todd said. "Why not relax and have a little fun?"

Sighing, Kara said, "See, this is what I mean. I don't want to marry anybody, but I do want to develop friendships. It's important to me that those friendships include Christ. Otherwise, it would be like a zebra dating a rhino. The only thing those two have in common is that they both have four legs."

Kara could feel Todd scowling through the phone. "Please understand," she begged. "It's not that I don't like you. I do. You're the most exciting guy I've ever known. I'm . . . I'm really sorry it has to be this way."

Todd's voice shook. "All right. But I'm having a hard time understanding. It seems to me that if two people like each other, then . . ." He sighed. "I've gotta go. See you around, Kara."

Kara squeezed her eyes shut. Capturing the tears before they could fall, she continued to cradle the purring phone. Sometimes the price of following Christ was high. If only she and Todd could stand on Christ's love. If only there were a way.

Matters of the heart can be so complicated. Help me establish good friendships with Christian guys who love You. And, Lord, if there are no Christian guys to be found, send a revival to my school and hurry!

Additional Scripture reading: 2 Corinthians 6:15–18

THE
TRYOUTS

But seek first the kingdom of God and His
righteousness, and all these things shall be
added to you.—Matthew 6:33

Kara and Jenni were sharing a giggle when Dee Ann breezed
into their midst. Breathlessly, she announced, "Kara, I wanted to
tell you about an opening on our cheerleading squad. We're having
tryouts a week from Friday. I thought you'd like to compete for the
position!"

Shielding her eyes from the sun, Kara confessed, "I've never
been very good at popularity contests."

"It's not based on popularity. It's based on skill. I thought you'd
like to come out to practice this afternoon and learn a few cheers."

Kara looked at Jenni's pouting face. "Uh, can Jenni come, too?"

"Sure. Everyone is welcome."

Jenni asked, "This is already the fourth week of school. Why is
there an opening now?"

Checking for eavesdroppers, Dee Ann lowered her voice. "Jackie
Shelton is pregnant."

"You're kidding!" Kara said with a gasp. "Is she very far along?"

"Three months. She can't hide it anymore, and she refuses to
get an abortion."

"That's good," Kara said. "At least she's doing the right thing."

"I'm not so sure," Dee Ann confided. "Her whole life is up in
the air. The cost of her decision seems a little high to me. The baby's
due in February, and there are so many unanswered questions."

"Unanswered questions, like what?" Kara asked.

"Well, like, will she marry the father? Will she be able to finish
her senior year? She had planned to go to college to study art, but

that seems impossible now. It's sad." Dee Ann sighed before riveting her eyes on Kara. "So, how about joining us at 3:30 on the football field? You might even get to see Todd practice!"

Kara's stomach churned. "Uh, let me think about it. I've never pictured myself as cheerleader material."

"You'd be great!" Dee Ann encouraged, waving at Matt who stood with his friends across the school yard. "I've got to run. Let me know what you decide."

Jenni studied Kara hard. "You wouldn't," she challenged.

"I don't know. It's an interesting thought," Kara admitted. She studied Jenni. "Let's both go to practice this afternoon. It would be great exercise. Besides, how do I know you wouldn't beat me out?" Kara teased. "Then I'd be able to boast, there goes my friend, Jenni—the cheerleader."

Jenni giggled. "Now that you put it that way, it doesn't sound so bad. Maybe those years of ballet lessons will pay off."

Sizing up her competition, Kara said, "Yeah, they just might. I've never had the chance to test my coordination. You might be tough to beat." Kara patted Jenni's back. "Besides, I think you'd make a great cheerleader!"

When interesting opportunities come my way, help me to stop and ask for Your guidance. If You want me to go ahead, show me an open door; if not, close the door. But help me remember what I asked You if I should bump into a closed door. Remind me not to pick the locks.

Additional Scripture reading: Psalm 32:8–11

PRACTICE PERFECT

Do not let your adornment be merely
outward . . . rather let it be the hidden person
of the heart, with the incorruptible beauty of
a gentle and quiet spirit, which is very
precious in the sight of God.—1 Peter 3:3–4

Kara tried to keep her eyes focused on the cheerleaders and not on the football field. Seeing Todd work out with his team ripped her apart. *If only things could be different.*

Swishing a pair of pom-poms through the air, Kara shouted, "Two bits, four bits, six bits, a dollar, all for the Eagles stand up and holler!"

Kara leaped into the air, feeling like an idiot. Her legs and arms almost followed her bidding but missed the precision captured by the others.

Kara noticed Jenni looked as if she were born to cheer. Her bouncing blond curls and her slimming waist were accented by perfect poses and jumps. Jenni's ballet lessons were indeed paying off.

Once again, Kara diverted her attention to the football field, missing a synchronized handclap. *If only I could keep my mind on these cheers,* she scolded herself, watching Todd watch her. Todd dropped the football, and Kara missed another hop.

After practice, Dee Ann stopped Kara as Jenni went ahead to the locker room.

"Kara, that was a good first try. All you need is a little work."

"A *lot* of work, you mean," Kara teased.

"Why don't I come over tonight and we'll go over a few cheers? You'll get the hang of it. You'll see."

"That would be great. Would you mind if Jenni came?"

"That's fine with me, although she is your competition."

"I wouldn't feel right about leaving her out," Kara confessed. "Jenni did great today. She might have a chance to make the team."

"She's good," Dee Ann admitted. "Has she lost some weight?"

"Yeah!" Kara boasted, proud that Dee Ann had noticed. "We both have."

Dee Ann appraised Kara with her eyes. "Well, don't overdo it. You look just right."

"I'm almost there," Kara said.

Dee Ann laughed. "Kara, if you lose any more weight, we won't be able to find a cheerleading skirt to fit you!"

Kara smiled, secretly hoping that Dee Ann was right. She'd love to be noticed as the girl who had totally conquered her weight problem.

Help me have a balanced attitude about my body. I know it's important to stay in shape, but it's also important not to get hung up about my size. Help me love myself, no matter what shape I'm in.

Additional Scripture reading: Psalm 31:8–16

HARD QUESTIONS

Jesus answered, "My kingdom is not of this
world."—John 18:36

Kara was still practicing long after Jenni and Dee Ann had gone
home. "Two bits, four bits, six bits, a dollar . . ."

"Kara," her mom called from the kitchen, "you never finished
your dinner. Shall I pop it in the microwave for you?"

"I'm really not hungry," Kara replied.

Her mom stuck her head into the living room and studied Kara
with a frown. "All right. I'll slip it into the refrigerator for later.
Promise me you'll eat, okay?"

"Sure," Kara answered, punching the air in timed perfection.
"When I'm through practicing."

The phone rang, and Kara grabbed it before Bryce had time to
abandon his homework.

"Hello?"

"Hi, Kara. This is Todd. I saw you working out with the cheerleaders today. Are you trying out for the squad?"

"Yeah. Jenni, too," Kara answered.

"That's great," Todd said. "I hope you make it." His voice tensed,
"I know you don't want to go out with me. But I just can't get you
off my mind. I've never had a girl turn me down for a date. It's got
me wondering."

Kara's heart continued its aerobic beat. She asked, "What
about?"

"This faith of yours. I'm trying to figure out why it's so important
to you. Could I ask you something?"

"Sure."

"Well, if there is a God, why is there so much suffering in the world? Why are children starving in Africa? Why are there calamities like hurricanes and earthquakes?"

Gulping, Kara answered, "I don't know for sure. But I do know this world's not perfect. It was at one time, but people's sins changed all that." Kara sighed, trying to think of a way to explain. "Much of the suffering today is brought about by our own choices."

"What do you mean?"

"Well, take world hunger. When's the last time you sent money to help a starving family in a developing country?"

"Never, I guess," Todd admitted.

"Do you realize that the world has enough resources to feed every hungry man, woman, and child? Many people and organizations do what they can to help, but their efforts fall short of the needs. Is that God's fault?"

"I guess not. But what about natural disasters, like 'acts of God,' that kill and destroy?"

"Much of the blame is misplaced. Many of our troubles are actually brought about by our enemy, Satan."

"Well, why doesn't God stop him and fix the problems?"

"I think if God did that, we'd take Him for granted. We'd never search for Him. He'd mean nothing to us but a forced relationship."

"So?"

"Well, how would you feel if God forced Himself on you?" Kara answered for him, "You wouldn't love Him. You'd only fear Him."

"So, you're saying God *won't* answer our prayers?"

"No! God *does* answer but not always in the ways we ask. God's love is always there, along with His compassion and mercy. He'll help us to overcome, even when our world is crumbling around us. He's always there to give us hope. And I think that's worth a lot."

It's hard to figure out why You're so good and the world is so bad. I know that although You are not of this world, You love the world and sent Your own Son to die for us. You never force us to follow You. You love us enough to let us go into the world, and You love us enough to let us come home to You. Thank You for that kind of love.

Additional Scripture reading: John 3:17–21

❖

BLACKOUT

Have mercy on me, O Lord,
   for I am in trouble;
My eye wastes away with grief,
Yes, my soul and my body!
   —Psalm 31:9

"Push 'em back! Push 'em back! Way back!" Kara yelled, synchronizing her movements to match those of her cheering mentors. At last, her lanky arms and legs were snapping into position. Kara strained to perfect her cheers, and her heart beat hard against her chest. Again, she shouted, "Push 'em back! Push 'em back!" Suddenly, the world went black and Kara sagged to the ground.

"Kara!" Jenni screamed. "What's wrong? Are you all right?"

Kara tasted blood in her mouth. *I must have bitten my lip in the fall.* Her arms shook as she tried to sit up. The other girls crowded around her.

"Move back and give her some air!" Coach Joyce Lovett shouted, kneeling beside Kara.

Kara tried to focus on Coach Lovett's double image.

"Are you okay?" Coach Lovett asked, watching Kara blink.

Before Kara could answer, Jenni volunteered, "Kara studied through lunch today. I don't think she's had anything to eat."

The coach unpeeled a banana she had been saving in her fanny pack and gave it to Kara. "Your blood sugar's low. Here, eat this. It'll boost your sugar level."

Grasping the banana, Kara pulled her trembling legs into a standing position before collapsing onto the bench. Why did her body feel so out of control? "I'm sorry," she apologized to the gawking girls. "I'll be okay."

Staring at the fruit, Kara frowned. She nibbled a small bite. She hated to gorge herself on these calories. But she had no choice.

The coach sat down next to her. "Kara, you're not on a diet, are you?"

"Not really," Kara lied, unwilling to admit the truth, even to herself. "I've just been practicing too much, I guess. By skipping lunch, I ran out of gas."

"Over the years, I've seen some of my best cheerleaders leave the squad because of eating disorders, like anorexia. You're not trying to starve yourself, are you?"

Kara looked horrified. "No! Of course not! I just overdid it. That's all." She took a bite of the banana to emphasize her sincerity. "I'll be fine, really!"

"Stay on the bench for now. You can practice again tomorrow," the coach said, patting Kara's back. "And take care of yourself. You've really improved the last few days. The girls like you, and I think you may have a good chance at making the team. Don't blow it, okay?"

Kara nodded, surprised by the coach's revelation. "I'll do my best, Coach. Thanks."

Sometimes I feel out of control—as if my weight is the only thing I can control. When I feel like this, help me to give my size to You, so I won't overeat or undereat. I don't want to let worries about my shape consume me. Help me rest in Your peace, and give me wisdom when it comes to the food You would have me eat.

Additional Scripture reading: Romans 6:1–7

❖

THE WALL

My son, give me your heart,
And let your eyes observe my
ways.—Proverbs 23:26

Kara took an occasional bite and pushed her food around her plate, still feeling guilty about compromising her diet at cheerleader practice. She knew she couldn't afford another scene like the one she had created this afternoon. But she hated to blow it now, especially when she'd already lost ten pounds in such a short time.

Her thoughts were interrupted by the ringing of the phone. *Let it ring,* she thought, sighing, too tired to race Bryce.

"I've got it!" Bryce called, knocking his chair over in his mad dash. "Kara, it's that boyyy again."

Kara flushed and rose to retrieve the receiver, feeling a little light-headed.

She shut the door behind her. "Todd?"

"I saw you fall in practice today. Are you okay?"

"Yeah, that will teach me to skip lunch," Kara said, leaning against the wall.

"Oh?" Todd sounded surprised. "Well, I'm glad that you're okay."

Todd paused. "Kara?"

"Yes?"

"I've been thinking a lot about what you said the other night, and I was wondering if I could ask you something?"

"Sure," Kara answered, clenching the phone tighter.

"This question may not have an answer, but . . ."

"Go on."

"Well, if there is a God," Todd asked, "do you think He could make a wall so strong and high that nothing could break it?"

"Of course!"

"Then if God's so powerful, would He be able to break through the wall?"

Kara gulped. "I think so."

"But why isn't He powerful enough to build a wall that could withstand even Him?"

Kara felt dizzy. *Lord, what's the answer?* she prayed, waiting. The solution that flashed through her mind seemed simple, almost too simple. "Todd," Kara started, "I think God has already built a wall like that."

"He has?"

"Yeah, you don't have to go very far to find it. All you have to do is to look into your heart."

"What do you mean?"

"God made the walls of your heart so strong they can be taken only by force. But God won't break them, although He could if He wanted. God is polite. He'll wait outside until you invite Him in."

The line resounded with silence as Todd considered Kara's answer. "That makes sense," he finally said. "I guess that leaves me with one more question."

"What's that?" Kara asked.

"Do you think I could go with you and Matt to your next youth group meeting at your church? I'd like to hear more about God and His Son, Jesus."

Smiling, Kara answered, "Can you be ready Friday night at seven?"

When it comes to You, Lord, You give us freedom of choice. You will never force us into anything, but You will always be there, patiently waiting for us to follow You. Give me the courage to open wide the door of my heart to You.

Additional Scripture reading: Romans 10:8–13

THE COMPETITION

But Ruth said:
"Entreat me not to leave you,
Or to turn back from following
    after you;
For wherever you go, I will go. . . .
Your people shall be my people,
And your God, my God."—Ruth
    1:16

As the rest of the cheerleading contestants suited up in the locker room, Kara and Jenni sat watching the football team practice. A cool breeze splashed against Kara's damp forehead, and she asked, "Jenni, are you ready for this?"

Shrugging, Jenni answered, "I guess so. I feel confident of the cheers, but I still have my concerns."

"Why?"

"I guess I'm worried that one of us will actually make the squad."

Kara pushed her hair out of her eyes, watching Todd catch a pass. "Would that be so bad?" she asked.

"Kara, there's only one slot open. If one of us makes it, one of us won't. I don't know which scenario I'd hate more."

Shaking her head, Kara watched the other contestants scurry toward them. *Suzie and Beth look sharp in their bright T's and shorts. They're talented, perhaps the best. This contest will be interesting indeed.*

A few minutes later, Dee Ann was ready to lead the cheers, and the team captain, the coach, and a local dance instructor sat on the sidelines with their pens and score cards.

Dee Ann smiled at the five competitors and said, "Today you'll be judged on your smiles, poise, and performance." Dee Ann winked at Kara. "Take a deep breath and follow me. Let's start with 'Go, Eagles.'"

Kara's muscles tensed into position. Her heart thumped in anticipation as she suddenly realized how much she wanted to win.

"Go, go!" she shouted, projecting her best smile. "Get 'em, get 'em! Fight, Eagles, Fight!" She ended the cheer with a bouncing victory yell.

Out of the corner of her eye, she could see Jenni's flawless performance and graceful jumps.

Dee Ann announced the next cheer. "'Victory Cry' is next. Ready? V-I-C-T-O-R-Y, victory, victory is our cry!"

Kara felt her arms and legs snap into perfect form. She felt good. Really good. Oops! She missed a turn but caught up. She could see the judges scribbling on their pads.

Soon, the competition was over. She had done well, except for the goof. *It's hard to know how the others did. They were all behind me, except for Jenni. Jenni's cheers were perfect.*

Kara gave her friend a quick hug. "Jenni! You did great!"

Jenni's eyes misted. "Thanks, I think."

"What's wrong?" Kara asked.

"Us," Jenni answered. "Somehow I think this competition is going to split apart our friendship."

"We won't let it!" Kara said, putting her arm around her friend. "Let's make a pact now. We'll stay best friends, no matter what!"

Jenni faced the afternoon sun. "I know I would include you, Kara. But would you include me?"

Nodding, Kara watched the breeze dance with Jenni's curls. "In these last few weeks, I've learned a lot. One thing is sure, Jen, I need you. I'm not as strong a Christian without you."

Jackie Shelton, the former cheerleader, walked up to the girls. She flipped waves of red hair behind her back as she turned to Jenni. Her green eyes sparked. "I know I'm not one of the judges, but you did really well, Jenni. The best, I think." Jackie turned in time to see Kara's frown. "You did well, too, Kara. It'll be a close call."

Lord, send me friends who know You. It's so hard to go it alone. Help us to support each other in our stand for You. And if there is no one around who loves You, help me to share my faith in a way that will bring others to You.

Additional Scripture reading: Ecclesiastes 4:7–12

❖

THE WINNER

—

Whoever desires to become great among you, let him be your servant.—Matthew 20:26

Five hopeful girls sat around the locker room, waiting for the judges to tabulate their scores. Kara and Jenni huddled, too, full of emotion, speechless. The door to the coach's office cracked open. "Jenni? Kara? May I see you for a moment?"

The girls looked at each other while the team captain, Sandy, brushed past them with the final tally. Sandy quickly tacked it to the locker room bulletin board and hurried back into the coach's office.

As Kara and Jenni followed Sandy in, they could hear shrieks and moans as the other contenders read the results. *What's happening?* Kara wondered. Coach Lovett shut the office door and motioned for the girls to sit.

The judges shifted uneasily as the tension built. *Why are they taking so long to tell us which one of us made the team?* Coach Lovett finally spoke. "I called you in to tell you the results personally. The scoring was close. Almost too close. Jenni, you scored higher in the area of performance, but, Kara, you did better in poise and projection. So, the results were almost tied. The winner won by a half point." The coach looked at Kara and smiled. "Congratulations, Kara. You're the newest Summitview High cheerleader!"

Kara's mouth fell open. "Me?" She turned to Jenni, who slumped beside her.

Coach Lovett faced Jenni. "It was a close call. You did well, too. In fact, we've decided to ask you to be our alternate. That means you'll work out with the squad, and if anyone gets sick or if anyone else," Coach Lovett cleared her throat, "has to leave the squad for any reason, you can take her place. How do you feel about that?"

Jenni brightened. "You mean, I'll be a part of the squad?"

The coach smiled. "That's the sum of it. You'll only be performing occasionally, although you'll still be required to practice with the girls after school. What do you say?"

Jenni hugged Kara. "Yes!"

The coach studied the pair and smiled. "I haven't told the other cheerleaders yet, so don't say anything about being selected as an alternate until I've spoken to them. Okay?"

When Jenni and Kara stepped out of the office, the locker room was almost empty, except for a couple of cheerleaders.

Brooke turned to Kara, all smiles. "Congrats, Kara."

Kara grinned. "Thanks!"

Jenni remained by Kara's side, smiling.

Brooke turned to her. "You can go now, Jenni. The losers have already left."

Reddening, Kara put her arm around her friend's shoulders. "Jenni's my friend. I say she's welcome to stay."

Brooke looked surprised. "I just thought . . ."

Kara laughed. "Just because I beat Jenni by a half point doesn't mean I'm going to dump her. We're a team that won't be broken, although we'll be happy to include you and the others if you care to join us."

Help me not to flake out on my friends if someone puts them down. Teach me that true friendship is about love and service. Remind me that all of the kids at my school have value. Help me share Your love with them, no matter where they stand in terms of popularity.

Additional Scripture reading: 1 Peter 1:22–25

❖

DIET WISE

Let us lay aside every weight, and the sin
which so easily ensnares us, and let us run
with endurance the race that is set before us.
—Hebrews 12:1

Slumped in her chair, Kara shared her news at the dinner table as she scattered her uneaten food. "Anyway, they were so impressed with Jenni, they're letting her be an alternate. So, we're both on the team!"

Mrs. Daniels passed the steaming rolls to Bryce and said, "That's great, Kara, I'm really proud of you. I'm also glad that you and Jenni are going to stick together. I was worried how she might take another failure."

"She's doing a lot better," Kara confided, wishing she didn't have to concentrate on conversation. "She's been memorizing that 'Who You Are in Christ' list I gave her. It's really helped."

Kara rolled a green pea from one side of her plate to the other. "Jenni used to feel worthless. She thought she had lost control over her life. But now she's given that control to God."

Matt, who had been studying Kara's table maneuvers, said,

"That's great, Kara. But why haven't you tried Mom's lasagna? It's really good tonight."

"I *am* eating it. It's delicious!" Kara defended, pressing a creamy bite to her lips.

Bryce laughed. "Fibber! I've been watching you. You haven't eaten a bite."

Flushing, Kara responded, "This cheerleading tryout made me too nervous to eat."

"Is that why you fainted during practice yesterday?" Matt asked. "Dee Ann told me about it."

"What?" Mrs. Daniels asked. "You fainted? I've been concerned about you lately. Have you been feeling all right?"

"I feel great," Kara gushed.

Kara's parents exchanged glances. Mr. Daniels spoke, "Kara, your mom and I have been worried about you. You seem so tired, you never eat, and you're always practicing your cheers. Are you on some sort of diet?"

"Jenni and I lost a few pounds," Kara admitted. "We just wanted to get in shape."

"How much weight have you lost?" her dad asked, concern clouding his eyes.

"Twelve pounds so far," Kara boasted.

Mr. Daniels frowned. "So what do you weigh?"

Fidgeting with her food, Kara answered, "I don't know."

"If you know you've lost twelve pounds, you do know," Mr. Daniels countered. "Tell me."

Dropping her gaze, Kara answered, "I guess I weigh about 106 pounds."

Mrs. Daniels gasped and rose to retrieve a brochure from a nearby drawer. As she scanned it, she said, "Kara, you're five six. According to this chart, a five-six, sixteen-year-old girl can weigh up to 132 pounds without being overweight. Anything under 116 pounds is underweight!"

"I think I look better at *this* weight!" Kara challenged.

"More like a skeleton," Bryce quipped, "great for a Halloween date!"

Mrs. Daniels glared Bryce a warning, and Mr. Daniels said, "Kara, after dinner tonight, I'd like to have a talk with you . . . alone. All right?"

Kara bit her lip. "Okay," she answered, knowing it was useless to argue.

Twelve pounds, she mused. *What's the big deal?*

Lord, help me to get my identity not from how I look but from who I am in You. For You have given me a new identity based on Your love for me, not based on the world's standards. Help me to see myself as You see me—pure, clean, and beautiful, clothed in Your love.

Additional Scripture reading: Romans 6:13–18

❖

DIET CRASHED

Do not look at his appearance or at his physical stature. . . . For the LORD does not see as man sees; for man looks at the outward appearance, but the LORD looks at the heart.
—1 Samuel 16:7

After dinner, Mr. Daniels said, "I would like everyone to leave Kara and me alone."

Bryce pushed his chair under the table and sang, "Kara's gonna get it!"

Mrs. Daniels put her hand on Bryce's shoulder and guided him out of the kitchen. Matt followed.

Mr. Daniels cleared his throat. "Matt's right, Kara. You've stopped eating. Do you want to tell me about it?"

"There's nothing to tell, other than what I've already said," Kara defended. "Jenni and I cut back a little on our food intake and lost a few pounds."

"What I don't understand is why you thought you were overweight," Mr. Daniels said.

"The guys at school said I was fat," Kara said, studying the deep wrinkles of her father's frown. "At first, I thought they were just being crude, but then I noticed that I did have a little flab on my stomach. That's when I decided they were right."

"Kara, don't let rude remarks govern your actions. Girls *should* have more body fat than boys. You certainly weren't fat when you started your diet, and now you're underweight."

Kara's voice whined in protest. "How can you say that? I still have a few pockets of flab left to lose!"

"What flab? You're a young woman, and you're attractive just as you are."

"It's just that I want to be perfect," Kara admitted.

"Excuse me. Did you say *perfect?*"

Kara nodded. "What's wrong with that?"

"First, weight is not a characteristic of perfection. And second, you and I both know that only one person was ever born perfect. Are you trying to take His place?"

"I could never take Christ's place. I only meant, I want to *try* to be perfect."

"Perfectionism is a lofty goal, Kara, but an impossible one. The only true test for perfectionism is this: Can you forgive yourself? Kara, you need to see yourself through the eyes of the heavenly Father who loves you. When Jesus said, 'Love your neighbors as yourself,' He didn't mean, 'Love only your neighbors but not yourself.'"

"I know that."

"But you're not living as if you believe it."

Mr. Daniels adjusted his glasses. "Let me ask you a question. If I gained fifty pounds, would you still love me?"

"Of course," Kara answered, pushing her plate away. "I might not feel good about your weight, but I'd still love you."

"Well, let's pretend *you* gained fifty pounds. Could you still love yourself?"

"I don't know."

"You should love yourself, regardless of your weight," Mr. Daniels said as he looked into Kara's eyes. "I think I need to reemphasize the fact that you're *not* overweight! You've been viewing yourself through mental glasses that create an optical fat illusion. You think you're fat; therefore, that's how you see yourself. Dieting is not going to help your self-image. When you get caught in this kind of disillusionment, you can't see yourself objectively. Kara, your so-called diet is not getting you in shape. It's destroying your healthy body."

Lord, if there is some area in my life that I'm trying to control, I give it to You. Help me understand that I'll never be perfected through my own efforts. Yet You see me as perfect through the efforts of Jesus Christ, Your Son. I renounce any attempt to earn my own way to You. I submit to Your love and forgiveness.

Additional Scripture reading: Romans 8:5–11

DIET BALONEY

"Not by might nor by power, but by My
Spirit," says the LORD of hosts.—Zechariah 4:6

"Can't you see? Your efforts to perfect yourself through dieting are baloney. Just like Jenni, you need to understand who you are in Christ. Your identity isn't based on your appearance or even your ability to control your circumstances. It's based on God's love for you. Can you understand that?"

Kara stared at her plate of cold food. "I think so."

"Hating your body because it doesn't conform to your idea of beauty tells me you hate yourself. That's wrong."

Kara's dad arched his brows as his brown eyes glowed with concern. "Do you still have that list telling you who you are in Christ—the one you gave to Jenni?"

"I remember most of it, I think."

"Can you list some of those attributes for me?"

Sighing, Kara counted off her fingers. "Let's see, when I'm in Christ, I am accepted, loved, and significant; my old nature is removed; I'm a new creature; and God will never leave me or forsake me."

"That's good, for starters. But I would like you to memorize the entire list and quote it to me next week. It's important you understand that those attributes apply *even* to you. Will you do that for me?"

"I guess so."

"Good, in the meantime, I think we've caught your problem soon enough before any real damage was done."

"Damage?"

"Fasting and purging will destroy your health, rot your teeth, cause dehydration and starvation, and eat away your heart muscles. That's how Karen Carpenter died."

"The singer?"

"Yes. She was trying to recover from an eating disorder and was already back on a healthy diet. But her heart, horribly damaged from the abuse her body had endured, simply gave out."

"I had no idea there were side effects like that."

"That's why it's so important that you get back on a proper diet, starting tonight."

"But, Dad, the thought of cramming all that food into my mouth makes me want to puke. I don't think I can do it."

Kara's dad pushed her plate toward her. "When a person stops eating, like you have, the eating mechanisms shut down and have to be turned on again. I'm not surprised to hear that you don't feel like eating. That's the very reason you *must* eat. I'll sit here with you and encourage you."

Kara gulped and looked at the uneaten lasagna strewn around her plate. As she fumbled for her fork, her vision clouded. "I can't, Dad. I really can't."

"Do it anyway," Mr. Daniels said. "One bite at a time."

Sliding a bite between her teeth, Kara felt she would suffocate. She chewed slowly, unable to salivate.

"Keep trying," Mr. Daniels encouraged.

Kara gagged, swallowing the rubbery noodles.

"I know it's unpleasant, but your body will thank you. Soon, you'll be able to appreciate and even enjoy your food again."

(To be prayed aloud.) *I renounce starving myself as a way to gain control over my body and life and announce that I am handing that control over to Jesus Christ.*

"I renounce vomiting to purge myself of evil and reject the lie that my self-worth is based on my physical appearance. I announce that all food created by God is good and that nothing is to be rejected by those who know the truth.

"I renounce taking laxatives and defecating to purge myself of evil. I announce that it's not what enters my mouth that defiles me but what comes from the heart.

"I renounce cutting myself to purge myself of evil. I announce that only the blood of Jesus can cleanse me."—Quoted from Neil T. Anderson and Steve Russo, *The Seduction of Our Children* (Eugene, Oregon: Harvest House, 1991) 223.

Additional Scripture reading: Romans 8:1–4

CLASSROOM GODS

Beloved, do not believe every spirit, but test
the spirits, whether they are of God; because
many false prophets have gone out into the
world.—1 John 4:1

A few days later, at the closing lunch bell, Kara waltzed into her
English class. *That cheeseburger was good,* she thought, gliding into
her chair.

Kara shuddered. *What would have happened if Dad hadn't forced
me to see what I was doing? When would I have quit lying to myself?
When would I have stopped hurting my body?*

When the bell rang, Coach Lovett erased the blackboard and
announced, "Today, I want you to imagine that this blackboard is
your mind. I want you to erase all of your thoughts in an effort to
get in touch with your personal spirit guides."

Kara gulped. *Spirit guides?*

The coach continued, "This exercise will teach you how to allow
the universe to access your mind and help you free yourself into
powers that will knit your consciousness to nature's consciousness."

Kara squirmed in her chair.

"Your assignment is to close your eyes, erase your thoughts, and
wait for a being, or spirit guide, to greet you. Ask this being three
questions: Who am I? How do I fit into the scheme of things? And
where do I go from here? Write the answers on a sheet of paper
and turn them in to me."

Here comes another adventure, Kara thought, raising her hand.
"Coach Lovett, I would like to be excused from participating."

Coach Lovett swiped her straight blond bangs out of her eyes
and glared at Kara. She flipped her long braid behind her back.

"This is a simple exercise that will expand your creativity. Why do you want to be excused?"

Kara explained, "I . . . I don't believe in talking to spirits."

"Some people think that talking to spirits is a mind-expanding activity," Coach Lovett responded. "Many of my former students have found that getting in touch with the oneness of the universe is very helpful. I want you to reap the same benefits."

"I'm sorry, but I can't. Besides, I believe that this exercise is illegal."

Kara held her breath, watching uncertainty flash across Coach Lovett's face.

Coach Lovett's voice held steady. "Kara, there is nothing illegal about using your imagination in the classroom."

"But if we are talking with some sort of invisible life form, isn't that praying? The Supreme Court ruled that prayer in the classroom is illegal."

Coach Lovett flushed. "I disagree with your reasoning. But I suppose I will have to make allowances for you. Although I still want you to answer the three questions from your own perspective."

Dee Ann, who was sitting in the back of the room, raised her hand. "Coach Lovett, may I also be excused? I don't feel right about participating either."

"All right. Would anyone else like to try Kara and Dee Ann's alternative exercise?"

Kara blinked hard as a dozen hands sprang up from around the class. She smiled to herself, glad she had made a difference. But what would her boldness cost her with her cheerleading coach?

Jesus, help me not to be taken captive by strange ideas. Instead, teach me to recognize the difference between Your spirit and evil spirits. Teach me to slam the door shut before trouble creeps in. I want to deadbolt the spirit of deceit, but at the same time I want to be opened wide to Your spirit of truth.

Additional Scripture reading: 2 Corinthians 10:3–5

❖

THE
THREAT

—

Beware of false prophets, who come to you in
sheep's clothing, but inwardly they are
ravenous wolves.—Matthew 7:15

When the bell rang, Coach Lovett said, "Kara, I'd like to see
you at my desk."

Kara stepped forward as her classmates flowed around her like a
river.

Coach Lovett's dangling crystal earrings flashed rainbows that
seemed to ignite her steely gray eyes. "Kara, I don't understand
what you did in class today. You seemed to want to undermine my
efforts in leading the class in a helpful experience."

Kara's knees wobbled. "Coach, if you had said to imagine a
beautiful waterfall, then describe it . . . I would have. Or if you had
asked me to make up a dialogue, and write it down . . . I would
have. But you asked me to *talk* to a spirit guide. That's where I
draw the line. The spirit world is real and full of *real* demons."

"I'm surprised that you believe in a spirit world, especially after
just reading your narrow, fundamental worldview," Coach Lovett
snapped.

Kara cringed. "I *do* believe in the spirit world. But I believe that
spirit guides, spirits who talk in seances and through channelers,
are *liars!* I believe that these spirits are demons who want to trick
and hurt us. They'll hook us with just enough truth to capture our
imagination, then they'll brainwash us with lies. That's why I avoid
astrologers and fortune-tellers. I don't care what they might be able
to tell me. I don't want to get burned!"

"I would think that you would want to learn from these spirits,"
Coach Lovett said.

"I really don't need to talk with them. I talk to God. I know that He loves me and wants the best for me."

Coach Lovett rolled her eyes and crossed her arms. "I can't change your thinking, Kara, but I've found that my openness to spirit guides or masters of the universe has helped me be more willing to tolerate the differences of others."

"I believe that we shouldn't just *tolerate* others. We should *love* others, like Jesus taught. It's hard sometimes, but with God's help, it works."

"That's interesting, Kara," Coach Lovett said, tapping her long fingernails. "By the way, it might interest you to know that I've assigned Rodger Tracey to be your partner for your upcoming research project."

Kara stared at Coach Lovett in disbelief. "But I thought you said you were tolerant."

"I am. But because I saw you and Rodger arguing in the hall, I think this will be the *perfect* opportunity for us to see if you *really* love others."

A slight smile curled around Coach Lovett's lips. "Oh, and by the way, I forgot to mention when you were in my office, all *new* cheerleaders are on probation. Since it appears that you may have a problem with dieting, I want you to weigh in this afternoon. You will be suspended from the squad if you lose so much as two pounds."

Kara grimaced. "Don't worry, Coach Lovett. My weight is already on the upswing, along with my faith in God."

God, it's nice to know that unlike Lucifer, You won't trick or hurt me. I renounce any instance in which I may have been seduced into talking to demons. Shine Your truth on any deceptions that may have crept into my life and expose the ravenous wolves that may lie in wait.

Additional Scripture reading: Ephesians 6:10–18

PRODIGAL

—

**I am the door. If anyone enters by Me, he will
be saved, and will go in and out and find
pasture.—John 10:9**

Todd reached for Kara's hand as Jeff Hoffman, Summitview Fellowship's youth director, welcomed him to the group. Jeff said, "We're glad you came tonight, Todd."

Jeff, who was almost thirty, looked spunky in his jeans and "Christ Died for You" T-shirt. He scanned the crowd of about forty teenagers and said, "My topic tonight is God's love. How many of you believe that God really loves you?"

A shy wave of hands rippled the air. "Good," Jeff announced. "How many of you deserve that love?"

When no hands were raised, Jeff continued, "Tonight, I want to tell you a story that Jesus once told. . . . A certain man had two sons. They all worked hard on their family farm. But the younger son secretly plotted to leave. *After all,* he reasoned, *anything's gotta be better than a life of farm work.*

"One day, he approached his father. 'Dad, I've helped you build this farm, and now I'm ready to cash in, pick up my half of the inheritance, and travel to the big city to make my own way.'

"Reluctantly, the father mortgaged the family farm and gave his son his half of the money. The next day, the son packed his bags and left for adventure in the big city.

"At first, life seemed good to the young man. He had money, friends, and parties. That is, until his inheritance ran out. Deserted by his friends, he set out looking for work, but work was hard to come by.

"Finally, the young man found a job feeding hogs. He was so hungry, he almost ate the hogs' swill.

"One day, as he walked through the muck of the hog yard, he thought, *Even my father's hired workers have food to spare, and here I am starving to death. I will go home. I'll say, 'Dad, I've sinned against you and heaven. I am no longer worthy of being called your son. Make me one of your hired servants.'*

"Back home, the father kept a watchful eye on the road, always hoping for some word from his son. This day, as he turned to study the road, he saw a figure in the distance. It was his lost son! The farmer's heart was filled with compassion, and he ran to embrace his boy."

Jeff continued, "Let me read the rest of the story in the words of Jesus, found in Luke, the fifteenth chapter. The boy said, 'Father, I have sinned against heaven and in your sight, and am no longer worthy to be called your son.'

"But the father said to his servants, 'Bring out the best robe and put it on him, and put a ring on his hand and sandals on his feet. And bring the fatted calf here and kill it, and let us eat and be merry; for this my son was dead and is alive again; he was lost and is found.'"

Jeff looked up. "There is probably someone here tonight who is in a far country. You are away from your Father God, who loves you.

"Maybe you don't care. Your parties are too much fun. But be sure of this, life will catch up with you. Your bills will come due. Don't wait until that day.

"Turn your eyes toward home. God is waiting for you."

Todd shifted uneasily in his chair.

"God loves us so much that He sent His Son Jesus, whose death and resurrection created a door that joins God and us."

Jeff searched the crowd and his eyes rested on Todd. "Through Jesus, we can come home to God. Then, God can see us as whole, forgiven, and pure, no matter what we've done in the big city.

"Why die of starvation? Why not come home?"

I don't want to be on the run from Your love. Instead, give me the courage to enter in the door You have provided so that I can participate in the plans You have for my life.

Additional Scripture reading: John 10:7–15

TODD'S CHOICE

Simon Peter answered and said, "You
are the Christ, the Son of the living God."
—Matthew 16:16

Kara could feel Todd's grip tighten on her hand. Jeff searched
the faces of the young people. "Is there anyone here who is ready
to accept the Father's love and forgiveness?" he asked.

His eyes once again caught Todd's. Todd squeezed Kara's hand
tighter.

"Anyone?" Jeff asked again.

Kara's fingers ached from Todd's grasp. She prayed, *Lord, please
give Todd understanding and courage. Don't let him miss this opportunity to know You!*

"Everyone bow your head," Jeff instructed. "I sense that there
is someone here who has not yet decided to follow Christ. Please
don't wait. Life is short. You never know if you'll ever have another
opportunity."

Kara felt the imprint of Todd's class ring pressing its design onto
her fingers.

"If you would like to know Jesus as your Savior, please raise your
hand," Jeff said. "I'd like to talk to you for a few minutes."

Kara peeked through narrow slits to watch Todd's free hand. It
firmly gripped the seat of his chair.

Please, Jesus, she prayed, *please let Todd find You.*

Jeff sighed. "By the no show of hands, I trust that all of you know
the Lord. Let's take a refreshment break, then we'll play some games."

As the group broke up, Todd remained firmly planted in his chair,
staring at the ground.

"What is it?" Kara asked.

Todd could hardly speak. "It's what Jeff said, that story he told. It's like he was describing me."

Kara teased, "Are you a prodigal?"

Todd tried to swallow a lump in his throat. "I don't know, but I do know I've flunked Life 101 dozens of times. I've tried to do everything my way." Todd turned and looked into Kara's eyes. "I want that forgiveness Jeff talked about. I almost feel like this may be the only chance I'll ever get. But I'm not sure I'm ready for it. I just don't deserve it."

"None of us deserves what Jesus Christ offers us, don't you see? That was the whole point of Jeff's story tonight. We've all messed up. That's why Jesus died for us, to take the blame for the wrong things we've done."

Todd rocketed out of his chair. "I don't know, Kara. I've got to get some fresh air. This is too much for me to absorb."

Lord, it's hard to understand what You see in me. You've given so much, especially when I've given so little in return. Lord, all I have to give You is myself.

Additional Scripture reading: John 12:44–50

❖

CONNECTION

Blessed be the God and Father of our Lord
Jesus Christ, who according to His abundant
mercy has begotten us again to a living hope
through the resurrection of Jesus Christ from
the dead.—1 Peter 1:3

Kara followed Todd. "Wait up!" she called.

Todd broke through the front doors of the church and sprinted for his car.

"Todd, are you leaving?"

Whirling around, Todd begged, "Come with me, Kara."

"The meeting's not over. " Kara pleaded, "Won't you stay a little longer?"

Shaking his head, Todd said, "I just realized what I almost did. I almost made a commitment to follow Christ."

"Would that be so bad?" Kara asked.

"I don't know," Todd answered. "I feel so heavy. I just need to get away."

The church door swung open and Jeff Hoffman stepped outside. "Todd, Kara, come back in," he called. "We're about to start again."

Todd looked away as Jeff approached. "What's wrong, Todd?" Jeff asked.

"It's your message," Todd confessed. "It hit too close to home, you know?"

Jeff leaned against Todd's car. "I see. Would you like to talk about it?"

"Yes . . . I mean . . . no . . . well, I'm not sure."

"Asking Christ into your life and accepting His love and forgiveness are big steps," Jeff admitted.

"That's just it," Todd exploded. "I've got a lot of friends. They just wouldn't understand if I suddenly turned into a Bible worm."

"I understand what you're saying, but please don't let your friends keep you from knowing God," Jeff responded.

Todd started to open his car door. "I don't know. This is all so overwhelming."

"Todd, wait," Jeff said. "Let me ask you a question."

"All right."

"Do you believe that God loves you?"

"I do," Todd admitted. "I can feel it."

"Do you believe that Jesus is God's Son and that He died on the cross and rose again as a sacrifice for your sins?"

Todd stared at the door handle and nodded. "I do," he whispered.

"Then don't run away," Jeff encouraged. "Accept God's love. Allow Him to forgive you, okay?"

Todd closed his eyes and sighed deeply. "I do want to know God's love and forgiveness. But He seems so much bigger than I am. I'm afraid if I fall into Him, I'll drown."

Jeff chuckled. "God may be big, but He can still come into your life and be your Lord."

Todd's arms dropped to his sides and his head hung down. "All right," he said. "I give in to God. What do I need to do to be saved?"

"Talk to Him. Give Him your life. Ask Him to forgive you of your sins." Jeff put his arm around Todd and encouraged, "You need to do it now. Just pray."

Todd nodded and bowed his head. He whispered, "God, it's me. You know who I am. You know the things I've done." Todd's voice cracked, "Please forgive me." He sighed. "I give my life to You."

As Todd looked up, Kara gave him a hug. She whispered, "How do you feel?"

The tension in Todd's face melted as a new light shone in his eyes. "Something's happening," he said. "It's like I'm being made brand-new!"

Jeff laughed. "That's a good way to put it, Todd. You've just been born again. God is imparting His Holy Spirit into your life."

Todd laughed. "This feels great," he said. "Why didn't you tell me this would happen? I'd have become a Christian years ago!"

Jesus, I celebrate Your life in my life. Thank You for Your mercy and for Your Holy Spirit. I ask that Your love will continue to grow in my life and that it will spill over to others.

Additional Scripture reading: Galatians 3:10–14

NIGHT
OF DISCOVERY

Turn away my eyes from looking at worthless
   things,
And revive me in Your way.—Psalm 119:37

Todd was silent as he drove Kara to McGuffy's. Finally, he spoke,
"You know, Kara, what happened to me tonight was totally awesome.
I feel so new inside, so fresh!"

Kara smiled at his silhouette. "I'm glad, Todd. I'm really excited
for you."

Todd pulled into the parking lot. His face lit up in the glow of a
streetlight.

"I feel that there is so much to learn about my new faith. I don't
know where to start."

"Why not start with the Bible?" Kara suggested.

"Isn't that a pretty big book?" Todd asked, popping his door open.

Kara giggled as he opened her door for her, "If I were you, I'd
start with the book of John in the New Testament."

"Test-of-what?" Todd asked.

"Test-A-MENT," Kara answered. "It's the part of the Bible that was
written after Jesus' arrival as a man. Todd, do you even have a Bible?"

"Yes," Todd answered. "My grandmother gave me one for Christ-
mas. I only opened it long enough to see if she had hidden a check
between its covers."

"Did she?"

"No," Todd laughed. "So I thought, *This is worthless.* I put it
away on my shelf."

"Ahhh," Kara responded. "Now, you're about to discover what a
treasure the Bible really is."

When Todd and Kara received their order, Dee Ann called from a hidden cubbyhole, "Todd, Kara, over here."

Todd carried their tray and Kara followed, sliding next to Jenni.

Dee Ann said, "Matt, Jenni, Ryan, and I are heading for the movies. Do ya want to come? It starts in twenty minutes."

Kara hesitated. "What's playing?" she asked.

Dee Ann laughed. "Some horror flick. I think it's called *Gross Night of the Bloody Knife.*"

"Sounds lovely," Kara joked.

"It's gory," Dee Ann admitted. "Despite its rating, I don't think it has any naked bodies or anything. Come! It'll be fun."

Todd smiled. "Let's go, Kara. I feel like celebrating."

Kara thought for a moment. *If Matt's going to see it, it can't be that bad.*

Protect my eyes, for they are connected to my heart. Help me to point them at things that will keep me strong in You. Do not let worldly entertainment creep into my life and block my spiritual arteries. Revive me in Your ways.

Additional Scripture reading: Matthew 6:19–23

HORRORS

We do not look at the things which are seen, but at the things which are not seen. For the things which are seen are temporary, but the things which are not seen are eternal.
—2 Corinthians 4:18

Kara and Todd stood in the ticket line with Dee Ann, Matt, Jenni, and Ryan. Shivering in the night air, Kara whispered to Dee Ann,

"I try to avoid these flicks, especially the gory and sexy ones. I hope this one's okay."

"Do what I do when I'm at home with my parents . . . close your eyes in the bad parts," Dee Ann said with a laugh.

Kara stamped her feet, and her words swirled into a warm mist that curled into the cool air. "I don't know what's worse, seeing the bad parts or imagining them with the help of *surround sound.*"

"Well, I for one am excited," Dee Ann said.

Kara spotted Rodger Tracey, standing in line behind her. She wrapped her arms more tightly around herself. "Hi, Rodger."

Rodger glared at her. "Well, if it isn't Miss Tantrum Daniels. You're so far above the rest of us, I'm surprised to see you at a movie like this." He started to say more but noticed Todd's narrowed eyes.

Todd asked, "Kara, who's your friend?"

"This is Rodger Tracey," Kara said. "We have lockers next to each other."

Todd sized Rodger up and sneered, "Let me know if this little tick bothers you."

Kara reddened. *Wait till Rodger finds out we're going to be research partners,* she thought. *I'm doomed. He'll hate me forever.*

The movie started with a heavy love scene. Kara blushed. *I can't believe I'm sitting here with my date, watching this couple make out. I hope this doesn't send Todd the wrong signals.*

Later, as a gore-encrusted phantom thrust his blood-stained knife into the heart of a teenage girl, Kara stood up.

"Where are you going?" Todd asked.

"Out," Kara replied.

As Kara made her way to the aisle, she stepped on the toes of Rodger Tracey. He looked from the screen to Kara and snarled, "Hey, Babe, that's what I'd like to do to you."

Kara quickened her sidestep to the freedom of the aisle. Turning to look back, she was surprised to see Todd and Jenni following.

When the threesome entered the lobby, Jenni gasped, "Can you believe that garbage!"

Kara giggled and shook her head. "Sick! That's not what I want in my mind when I try to go to sleep tonight."

Todd asked, "So, what's the big deal? Haven't you ever seen a slasher movie before?"

"Not when I can help it," Kara admitted.

"Why not?" Todd asked. "What harm is there in it?"

Help me pick videos and movies that will entertain and educate and not tarnish my spirit. For like a computer, my subconscious retains all images and thoughts that enter my eyes and ears. Help me turn the switch so I can keep my mind and heart pure for You.

Additional Scripture reading: Philippians 4:4–9

❖

ARSENIC POWER

The lamp of the body is the eye. If therefore your eye is good, your whole body will be full of light. But if your eye is bad, your whole body will be full of darkness. . . . How great is that darkness!—Matthew 6:22–23

The three teenagers stood in the movie theater lobby. Jenni said, "It's too bad we had to walk out. I would like to have known how *Gross Night* ends."

"That's easy," Todd joked. "All of the teenagers get killed, except Tanya. In the end, she unmasks and kills the monster!"

Kara's mouth fell open. "You mean you've seen this before?"

Todd laughed. "Nope, it's just that these movies have the same plot. When you've seen one, you've seen them all."

"Then why do they keep making them?" Jenni asked.

"Because," Kara answered, "teens like them."

Todd asked, "So, what's wrong with that?"

"These movies are full of images that work on our spirits like poison," Kara said.

"Poison? What do you mean?" Todd asked.

"Todd, you're in my history class," Kara answered. "Do you remember how Mr. Bently said Napoleon Bonaparte died?"

"Yeah," Todd answered. "Scientists have speculated he was poisoned by a trusted friend after his defeat at Waterloo in 1815."

"What makes scientists think that?" Jenni asked.

"Because," Kara said, "they ran tests on Napoleon's hair and discovered it contained arsenic."

"That's right," Todd said. "The theory is that a friend slipped this tasteless poison into Napoleon's wine for a period of years. Napoleon grew weak and finally died."

Jenni asked, "So, Kara, what's this got to do with the movie?"

"Don't you see? The first dose of arsenic didn't kill Napoleon. Perhaps it didn't even make him sick."

"How do you know?" Jenni asked.

Todd answered, "Because according to my chemistry teacher, arsenic is a heavy metal. Once swallowed, it stays in your body forever. It builds into your tissues until you finally get sick. After a period of time, you can even die."

"The same is true of horror movies," Kara explained. "One dose is not going to kill you. But once this stuff is in your mind, you have allowed a portion of poison into your spirit."

Todd said, "You know, I feel like a little of the joy I felt when Christ entered my life tonight evaporated. Perhaps you're right, Kara. Perhaps it's better to avoid flicks that darken our spirits."

"Hi," Matt interrupted.

Kara looked up to see Matt and Dee Ann with Ryan at their heels. "What are you guys doing out here?"

"We got sick of the movie," Kara confessed.

"So did we," Matt said.

Dee Ann said, "I would like to have found out how it ends."

Kara replied, "Ask Todd. He knows the whole plot."

*I want to throw back the curtains of my heart to let in Your Son-
light. Throw back my blinders and help me bask in the warm
glow of Your love.*

Additional Scripture reading: Psalm 37:1–6

HER
ENEMY'S CAMP

This is My commandment, that you love one
another as I have loved you.—John 15:12

The moment Kara had been dreading arrived. Stepping into study
hall, she scouted for Rodger. She spotted him blowing his nose into
a hanky.

"Hi, Tantrum," he called to her as she approached. "I'm surprised you had the guts to show."

"I know you don't like me," Kara said. "But let's try to make
the best of this situation."

Kara continued, "We've got some catching up to do since you
were out yesterday. So, let's get down to business. Do you have an
idea for our research paper topic?"

"How about gross anatomy?" Rodger blurted. His freckles
danced on his pale skin. "Maybe I could even try a few experiments
on you. I got a lot of ideas from *Gross Night of the Bloody Knife.*"

Kara felt her temperature rise but kept her voice cool. "Very
funny. I was thinking about something like the evils of drug abuse."

Rodger laughed, pushing his dark hair out of his eyes. "I don't
think so."

"Well, how about the environment?"

"Yeah, that might be okay," Rodger agreed, blowing his nose.

Kara asked, "Got a cold?"

Rodger snickered. "What do you care?"

Kara flushed. "Listen, Rodger, about the other day. I've been meaning to apologize to you. I was a real jerk to yell at you like I did."

"You're not pulling that on me!" Rodger said, sneering.

Kara's eyes widened. "Pull what?"

"Your sweet talk. It might work on the other guys, but I can see right through it."

Kara strummed her fingers on the table.

Rodger continued, "You're nothing but a manipulative snip. You're trying to get me to do the research for both of us."

"With your grades?" Kara said with a frown.

Rodger glowered.

Biting her lip, Kara said, "I'm sorry. I shouldn't have said that. Look, if I promise to do my share of the work load, can we call a truce?"

Rodger studied Kara's face. "All right. I can't afford a failing grade," he sniffed.

"Allergies?" Kara asked.

Rodger smiled. "I'm not contagious, so don't worry about it. Let's just divide up the work, okay?"

"That sounds like a plan," Kara agreed. "Why don't we use this hour to look up as many articles as we can find on Denver's brown cloud? I think air pollution might be an interesting angle on our report."

Nodding, Rodger turned to stare at a passing girl.

Kara flagged his attention. "Let's meet back here in forty minutes and discuss what we've found. We'll decide where to go from there, okay?"

"All right. Sounds good to me."

"Oh, and Rodger . . ." Kara dropped her gaze. "I just want you to know, I'm praying for you to find God."

Rodger rolled his eyes. "Can the guilt trip. Your tricks don't work with me."

Lord, the reason You want us to forgive others is not because they need to be freed from our wrath but because we need to be freed from a bitter spirit. Help me stay willing to forgive and love others despite their offenses against me.

Additional Scripture reading: Matthew 5:21–26

❖

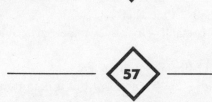

SNIFFING AROUND

Hatred stirs up strife,
But love covers all sins.
—Proverbs 10:12

A few days later, Kara and Rodger met in the library to compare notes. Kara was flipping through a text on pollution when Matt interrupted, "Kara, is everything okay here?"

"Oh, hi, Matt," Kara answered. "Rodger and I are going over our research project."

Matt's eyebrows shot beneath his dark curls. "Oh, that's . . . good."

Dee Ann breezed up to Matt and whispered, "Can I count on your vote?"

Smiling, Matt asked, "Vote? That depends. What are you running for?"

Kara interrupted the flirting. "Haven't you heard? Dee Ann's been nominated for Homecoming queen!"

Beaming, Dee Ann squeezed Matt's arm. "I'm so excited. The

big game is only two weeks away, and I've got to figure out what I'm going to wear!"

Rodger rolled his eyes at Kara. "Would you mind getting your little friends out of here so that we can finish this stupid project?"

Dee Ann turned, noticing Rodger for the first time. "We were just leaving," she snipped.

The couple walked away, arm in arm, while Rodger sneered. "Kara, your friends are airheads."

Kara looked up from an article. "Dee Ann? I think she's nice."

"A nice snob, you mean. Although I have to admit, I have enjoyed watching her bounce around in her cheerleading costume."

Looking up, Kara frowned. "What's that supposed to mean?"

"Haven't you noticed? Dee Ann's blossomed, you know, just like Jackie Shelton."

Kara slung her hair behind her shoulders and jotted a note on a card. "Oh, stop it, Rodger. You think everyone is fat. I think Dee Ann looks great."

Sniffing, Rodger tossed his hands into the air. "I'm just an outside observer. Besides, Brooke Kelly's getting a little chunky, too."

"Brooke is too gorgeous to be fat," Kara defended. She stopped and stared at Rodger. "Besides, I think you should worry about your own problems."

Rodger laughed and blew his nose into his hanky. "Oh, that's right, you said you're praying for me." He tucked his hanky into his pocket. "So, did God reveal any of my little secrets to you?"

Avoiding his eyes, Kara flipped through another book. "It's funny you should ask."

Rodger darted his eyes at Kara. "Yeah?" He looked intrigued. "What do ya mean?"

Kara reddened. "Well, I did pray for you . . ."

"And?"

"I'm embarrassed to even say anything."

"Say what?"

Her blush deepened. "It's just that I got this sense . . . it wasn't like I heard a voice or anything, but it was this strong sense that . . . never mind, it's too weird. I can't tell you."

"What?"

"Do you promise not to laugh?"

Rodger shrugged a nod.

Kara hesitated, "Well, when I was praying, I felt God was telling me that if you cleaned up your life, your sinus problems would clear up."

Rodger chuckled.

"I told you it was weird."

"Maybe not."

"Why do you say that?"

Rodger smirked. "Don't be so nosey, Kara."

When I'm praying and talking to You, teach me how to listen for Your still, small voice. Speak to me and teach me Your truths. But bind all voices of the Enemy from masquerading as You. Teach me how to love through strife.

Additional Scripture reading: John 15:9–17

❖

RALLY
BIG SURPRISE

I have set before you life and death, blessing
and cursing; therefore choose life, that
both you and your descendants may live.
—Deuteronomy 30:19

Feeling sheepish, Kara followed her mom and Jenni to the sidewalk that bordered the Summitview Women's Clinic. Sara Penrose and a small band of prayer warriors were already gathered, carrying their "Abortion Stops a Heartbeat" placards. Jenni noted a police K-9 unit in the center parking lot.

"Why are they here?" Kara asked Sara.

"They want to make sure no violence erupts. But they don't have to worry. None of us wants a violent confrontation," Sara responded. "Somehow, they must have gotten wind of our prayer venture."

Fear reflected in Jenni's eyes. "Will the police sic their dogs on us?"

"Not unless we commit a violent act or unless they want a lawsuit on their hands," Sara answered. "We will be safe. Just don't step off the public sidewalk onto the clinic's property."

Kara gulped and asked, "So what do you want Jenni and me to do?"

"Well, we're going to march around the sidewalk, silently, holding our signs and praying. A couple of other women and I will act as sidewalk counselors . . . counseling anyone who will talk to us. Prayer support is really important. You can start by praying for the teen who is already inside. Pray she won't abort her baby. Pray that the scheduled abortions will not take place, today or ever."

Jenni's blue eyes widened. "You say a teen is already in there?"

"Yes," Sara said sadly. "She went inside just as we were arriving . . . before we had a chance to talk to her. You probably know her. She was wearing a hooded green-and-white Summitview High sweatshirt."

Kara shuddered and exchanged glances with Jenni. "A hooded green-and-white sweatshirt? Only the cheerleaders have those," Kara said, a knot pulling tight in her stomach.

She eyed the police who were pacing the entrance with their German shepherds and shuddered again.

The praying protestors, about twenty strong, held hands. Sara's voice rang clear, "Lord, help our presence and our prayers make a difference today, for the unborn and for the young mothers who are scheduled to kill their babies."

Afterward, Kara silently paced the sidewalk with the other protestors.

Sara stood on the sidewalk beneath one of the clinic's windows. Tears streamed down her face. She called, "Please don't kill your baby. Come out. We love you. We're praying for you."

Kara and Jenni continued their silent march, hoping, praying, for the girl inside.

Soon the door of the clinic swung open. "Come back!" a voice called to a fleeing figure. "Choice is your right! Don't let them stop you!"

The girl continued to run. Kara turned and looked into her face. Stunned by recognition, she froze. Before she could think, Kara stumbled past the police dogs and ran to meet her friend.

Lord, You said You knew me as You knit me together in my mother's womb. Thank You for creating me. Help me realize that all human life is precious, a gift from You to us. Help our society choose life so our children can live.

Additional Scripture reading: Mark 10:13–16

❖

PREGNANT!

For nothing is secret that will not be revealed,
nor anything hidden that will not be known
and come to light.—Luke 8:17

Dee Ann's face was wet with tears. She staggered into Kara's arms. Hurriedly, the girls slipped by the police dogs, abandoning the cries of protest that pursued them.

When they reached the safety of the sidewalk, Dee Ann collapsed, sobbing. "I couldn't do it," she cried.

Jenni, Sara Penrose, and Joan Daniels surrounded the pair. Mrs. Daniels looked aghast. "You . . . you're Matt's girl, aren't you?"

Dee Ann continued to sob. "My life is ruined!"

Mrs. Daniels's voice trembled, "If Matt's responsible, we'll help you."

Dee Ann gasped for air, her shoulders quaking.

Kara raised her tear-streaked face over Dee Ann's shoulder and shook her head. "Mom, it wasn't Matt. Dee Ann was raped."

Jenni choked a cry and Dee Ann lamented, "If only it *was* someone like Matt instead of . . ."

Reaching for Dee Ann, Mrs. Daniels held her close. "Never mind," she whispered, stroking her hair. "We'll do whatever we can to help you. You'll get through this. You'll see."

"Dee Ann, do your parents know?" Sara asked.

Dee Ann wiped her eyes and shook her head. "That's the main reason I chose to have an abortion. They'll never understand." She sniffled. "How can I ever face them?"

Sara asked, "Would it help if we went with you to tell them?"

Nodding, Dee Ann said, "My dad won't throw me into the street if he has an audience."

Sara said, "If you need a place to stay, we have a network of volunteers who can help you. You really have a lot of options."

"And I've lost a lot of options," Dee Ann said, staring at the sidewalk. "Matt, the Homecoming court, the cheerleading squad . . . it's all over."

Kara hugged her friend. "Those things may be over for now, but your sacrifice will be worth your pain, you'll see. God will help you through this."

Dee Ann looked up through her tears. "Please don't tell Matt," she pleaded. "Not yet. Please, not yet."

Sometimes the sacrifice of doing the right thing is high. Sometimes it's higher than my ability to comprehend. But even so, I know You are with me. I know You go before me, and by Your hand You will help me overcome. You will turn my greatest sacrifice into my greatest triumph. You will bring the truth to light.

Additional Scripture reading: 1 John 5:1–5

ABORTED

Open your mouth for the speechless,
In the cause of all who are appointed to
die.—Proverbs 31:8

Dee Ann sat on the couch in the privacy of Sara's apartment, surrounded by Jenni, Sara, Kara, and Joan Daniels.

"Could I get you a glass of ice water?" Sara asked her.

Dee Ann shook her head, studying the tan carpet.

"How do you feel?" Kara asked, her eyes filled with worry.

"Confused," Dee Ann admitted. "When I went to Coach Lovett, she said that abortion was the best solution for rape."

"Many people believe that," Sara said. "I know."

Sara clenched and unclenched her fist. "When I was thirteen, I was raped. When my doctor told me I was pregnant, I cried. He patted my hand and scheduled me for an abortion. Everyone assumed it was the right thing for me. It was as if my baby was disposable because he happened to be biracial. The social worker said I couldn't bring a minority baby into the world. There were too many already."

Sara's voice cracked. "It was so unfair. No one asked me what I wanted. I loved my baby. The way his life came into existence wasn't his fault. He wasn't the one who committed a crime. But what was his punishment? Death."

Touching Sara's shoulder, Mrs. Daniels's eyes filled with compassion. "I didn't know."

Sara turned her head to hide her heartache. "The thing is, everyone expected my life to go back to normal . . . as if nothing happened. No one prepared me for the pain and nightmares that followed."

Rage filled Sara's voice. "Don't you see? My rape was dirty, violent. It made me feel guilty. Aborting my child was also a dirty, violent act. It, too, made me feel guilty. Instead of allowing something good to come out of my ordeal, I participated in my baby's *murder!*"

Dec Ann reached for a tissue. "That's just how I was feeling when I was waiting for the nurse. I could hear another abortion taking place in the next room," she said.

"Another girl was there besides you?" Sara asked, deflating.

Dee Ann hid her eyes. "Yes. I could hear the whine of the abortionist's vacuum. When the slurping noise began, the other girl screamed, 'Stop! Please don't kill my baby!'"

Shuddering, Dee Ann said, "That's when I realized they were going to pull my baby from my womb, piece by piece. I felt like I was about to be raped again. I *had* to escape."

"You did the right thing," Sara said. "You've given your child a precious gift, the gift of life."

"But what kind of life will my baby have?" Dee Ann asked. "I'm not ready to be a mother."

Sara asked, "Have you considered putting your baby up for adoption?"

Dee Ann shook her head. "It's funny. I was willing to kill my baby, but now I can't imagine handing it over to a stranger."

"But you wouldn't have to do that," Mrs. Daniels volunteered. "With all the open adoption choices these days, you can pick the parents and even stay in contact with your baby. The choice is totally yours."

"Really?" Dee Ann asked. "Are there many couples who want to adopt?"

"There are three couples in my Sunday school class alone," Mrs. Daniels said. "I don't want to pressure you, but the gift of adoption benefits both the baby and the mom. Young women who make adoption plans take a major step in their personal development. Plus they have a better chance of achieving a higher education."

"Just think, Dee," Kara said. "In less than nine months, you can start over. You can still follow your dreams."

"Yes," Mrs. Daniels agreed. "With adoption, your baby is less likely to be on welfare and will probably live a life of less stress and frustration."

Sara echoed. "It's a hard choice, but like Joan said, it's a gift. A gift of life, love, and a future."

Thank You for giving me the gift of my life. Help me spend it wisely. Help me not to squander it but to invest it in the lives of my friends and family. Thank You for creating me.

Additional Scripture reading: Romans 12:17–21

❖

DEE ANN'S PARENTS

—

"Do not be afraid of their faces,
For I am with you to deliver you," says the
LORD.—Jeremiah 1:8

Sara Penrose, Kara, and Joan Daniels exchanged worried glances as they stood with Dee Ann at her front door.

"We can come back later," Sara said.

"No," Dee Ann answered. "Both of my parents are usually in good moods on Saturday mornings. With you here to back me up, I think I can face them."

Kara asked, "Do you know what you're going to say?"

Dee Ann bit her lip and shook her head. "No."

Taking a deep breath, Dee Ann pushed open her front door, calling, "Mom, Dad, we have company!"

Mrs. Miller came to the door, wiping her hands on a dish towel. "Joan, Kara! What brings you out on a Saturday morning?"

Mrs. Daniels smiled and said, "Dee Ann invited us."

Shooting a questioning look at her daughter, Sandy Miller shuttled her guests to the living room. "Make yourselves at home. Charles is just finishing his shave." Dee Ann and her guests sat on the overstuffed gray floral sofa. Kara's eyes traced the tapestried pattern of a mauve flower, avoiding contact with Mrs. Miller, who studied the group with a fidgety smile.

Mr. Miller's large bulk suddenly filled the doorway. "Guests?" he asked. "The Danielses and Miss . . . ?"

"Penrose . . . Sara Penrose," Sara answered, rising to shake Mr. Miller's hand.

Mr. Miller shot his wife a questioning look. "So, what brings the three of you here at ten o'clock on a Saturday morning?"

Kara continued to trace the floral pattern, glad that they had dropped Jenni off on their way over.

Clearing her throat, Dee Ann said, "I . . . I invited them. I have something to tell you, and I need their support."

The Millers leaned forward in their stuffed chairs. Mrs. Miller asked, "Is something wrong?"

Dee Ann stared at the thick smoky blue carpet. "I don't know where to start. So, I'll tell you this, I ran into Sara and the Danielses in town this morning . . ."

"In town? Dee Ann, I thought you were upstairs asleep. What were you doing in town?"

"I was down at Twentieth and Vine and . . ."

Mr. Miller stiffened. "At the Summitview Women's Clinic?" He stared at Mrs. Daniels. "I think I'm beginning to understand. Is this about you and Matt?"

"No, Dad."

"What then?"

Dee Ann's lip quivered and Kara handed her a tissue. "Mom, Dad, the last time I was out with Jack Raymond . . . he . . . I . . . well, it's my fault. We'd been drinking and . . ."

"Drinking!" Sandy Miller blurted. She eyed Kara hard. "You and your friends drink?"

"No, I mean, Jack and I. It was a mistake."

Mr. Miller frowned. "Did something happen the night you and Jack were drinking?"

Dee Ann avoided his eyes and nodded. "I told Jack no. But he wouldn't listen. I never wanted . . ." Dee Ann looked up into her dad's questioning eyes. "Dad, I'm going to have a baby."

Mrs. Miller gasped while Mr. Miller stood up and walked to the window.

"I'm . . . I'm so sorry," Dee Ann said, her voice cracking.

Rushing toward her, Mrs. Miller held out her arms. Mr. Miller turned to Dee Ann's friends, and his voice shook with anger. "Thank you for coming. But I really think it's time you left. I don't need the whole world to know how I've failed as a parent."

Dee Ann collapsed into sobs. "I'm sorry, Daddy. It's not your fault! Please forgive me. Please!"

Give me the power to live my life in such a way that I inspire and encourage others. But if I should wound another, teach me compassion and sorrow. And if my compassion and sorrow do not mend the wounds I've caused, help me forgive myself and release the wounded to You.

Additional Scripture reading: Hebrews 13:5–6

❖

WOUNDED LOVE

Before I formed you in the womb I knew you.
—Jeremiah 1:5

Sara rose from her place on the sofa. "Mr. Miller, I know this has been hard for you to hear. But, please, don't blame yourself." Sara took a tentative step toward him.

"Your daughter is a brave young woman. Today, instead of taking the easy way out and killing her unborn baby, she chose to face you and her mother."

Mr. Miller continued to stare into the front yard, studying the grassy carpet dulled under an overcast sky. "Haven't I taught Dee Ann better than to drink and fool around with some punk?" he asked, stroking his balding head.

"Please don't point fingers," Sara coaxed. "That's what my father did when I was raped."

Turning to study Sara, Mr. Miller blurted, "*You* were raped?"

Sara hung her head. "One Sunday night, when I was thirteen years old, my father told me to come straight home from church. Instead, I walked to a friend's house. On my way home, I was attacked." Sara shook her head. "My father never forgave me.

"I was devastated," Sara continued. "I'd always been Daddy's little girl. Then, at a time I needed him most, he turned against me. I don't know which hurt me most . . . the brutal rape, the abortion, or my father's rejection."

Mrs. Miller stood up and walked toward her husband. "Listen, Honey," she said. "We can't turn our backs on Dee Ann. She's our daughter. She needs our support. It doesn't matter who's to blame."

Dee Ann joined her mother. "Daddy, I just wanted to fit in. I didn't know that drinking could be so . . . so wrong. I never expected this to happen."

Touching her dad's arm, Dee Ann said, "I should never have gone out with Jack, especially when I knew what he expected from me. And I should never have taken that drink. I'm so sorry to disappoint you. Can you forgive me?"

Mr. Miller turned to face his daughter. His eyes glistened as he held her close. "This is such a shock. I never thought anything like this would happen to you. You've always been such an easy child, so perfect."

Dee Ann sniffed. "Well, I'm not perfect. I've messed up. But as Kara says, my life doesn't have to be ruined. I guess I've added a new chapter, one I hadn't planned on, and one full of struggle, but a chapter with a beginning and an end."

Mrs. Miller added, "We'll write this chapter of your life to-gether . . . all three of us."

Kara, Mrs. Daniels, and Sara exchanged smiles and rose to leave.

Mrs. Daniels said, "Well, we can see that we're no longer needed. Just know that we'll be praying for you."

"Thanks. Thanks for coming. I'm sorry I blew up," Mr. Miller said.

Mrs. Daniels said, "It's okay. I know the news was quite a jolt."

Sara pressed a slip of paper into Mrs. Miller's hands. "This is my number," she said. "If Dee Ann needs to get away, to prepare for the birth, we have a network of people willing to help and even host her in their homes. And if you decide on putting the baby up for adoption, I know of a good agency to help with that, too."

Mrs. Miller nodded.

"We won't repeat anything that happened here today," Mrs. Daniels added. "We'll respect you and your privacy. No one will ever hear about Dee Ann's pregnancy from us."

Dee Ann asked, "You won't even tell Matt?"

"We'll leave that to you," Mrs. Daniels said.

Thank You, Lord, that You can mend a heart and heal a broken dream. Thank You that You are full of compassion and mercy. Help me show Your compassion to others as You've shown Your compassion to me.

Additional Scripture reading: John 14:23–27

THE CONFESSION

**Therefore I exhort first of all that
supplications, prayers, intercessions, and
giving of thanks be made for all men.
—1 Timothy 2:1**

Kara couldn't get Dee Ann out of her mind as she sat in study hall with Rodger Tracey.

"So, you're going to get your mom to type this up for us?" Rodger asked.

Kara jarred back to the present. "What? Oh, yes. She said she'd be glad to help. I don't plan to take typing until next year."

"I don't type either," Rodger admitted.

Something about Rodger's voice caused Kara to look up. She noticed that Rodger's face missed its usual sneer. A soft glow shone in his eyes.

"Rodger, you look almost human today. Do you feel okay?" Kara asked.

"Ouch!" Rodger said, with a friendly grin. "Somehow, I didn't expect an insult from you today."

"I'm sorry," Kara confessed. "But is everything all right?"

Rodger's eyes twinkled. "Yes, I'm feeling fine. At least since my sinuses cleared."

Kara's eyes questioned Rodger's. "Your sinuses? Does that mean . . . ?"

Lowering his voice, Rodger said, "Let me ask you a question. Did you happen to pray for me last Saturday night?"

Kara mulled the question. "No, I mean, yes. Come to think of it, when our youth group divided into small prayer groups, some of my friends and I prayed for you. Why?"

Rodger's voice edged with mystery, "Well, it was the weirdest thing. Last Saturday night, I lost my desire for my two-year cocaine habit."

"Cocaine!"

"Shhh!" Rodger said, looking around. "Keep your voice down."

"You've been on coke for two years?"

Rodger looked sheepish. "Not only that. I've been the local dealer. You'd be surprised who my customers are."

Kara eyed him suspiciously. "So why are you telling me? Aren't you afraid I'll nark on you?"

Rodger leaned back in his chair. "I ain't all that worried, Kara. I'm clean now."

Kara looked incredulous. "You're off coke, just like that?"

Rodger smiled. "You and your friends must know some strong prayers. Tell me. Exactly what *did* you pray?"

Wrinkling her nose, Kara said, "It was a simple prayer, nothing fancy. I think I said something like, 'Lord, help Rodger to straighten up his life.'"

Rodger looked disappointed. "That's all?"

Kara shrugged. "That's all, Rodger. But I guess God answered anyway. Do you know much about Him?"

"I grew up knowing Him," Rodger admitted. "My mom took me to church every Sunday. When I was eight, I asked Jesus to come into my life and forgive me of my sins. And He did, I guess. But somewhere along the way, I decided I didn't need Him anymore."

"Is that when you got into drugs?"

"Yeah, when I wasn't getting high on Jesus, I needed something else. First it was huffing."

Kara's jaw dropped. "You mean you sniffed aerosol can fumes?"

"Yeah, until one of my friends dropped dead. That's when I learned that huffing can cause brain damage and stop your heart. So I turned to coke. Coke seemed to work for a while, but it turned into a nightmare. It was a habit that controlled me. I snorted every morning before school, then again every evening. I had to start selling the stuff to support my habit." Rodger sighed in relief. "But I'm out of that now. Saturday night, I turned back to God and flushed my supply down the toilet."

"That's great!" Kara exclaimed. "But what are your customers going to do without you?"

"I guess they'll have to do what I did . . . find out how to get high on Jesus."

Rodger lowered his voice again. "You see, Kara, when you told me that God showed you my sinus problem would clear up if I straightened out my life, you were right on. I knew you didn't know about my habit. So I figured you really had heard from Him. To tell you the truth, I was glad. I was ready to listen."

Show me how to be still and listen for Your voice. In Jesus' name, I block the voice of the Enemy from tricking me. Give me the patience to wait on You and Your word. Help me lead others to Your word. Thank You for giving me opportunities to serve You.

Additional Scripture reading: Ephesians 1:15–19

❖

A DATE?

For wisdom is better than rubies,
And all the things one may
  desire cannot be compared with
  her.—Proverbs 8:11

Todd gently held Kara's hand and looked into her eyes, oblivious to the morning greetings in the crowded school yard. "So, Kara, I've been waiting for the right moment to ask you. Would you go to the Homecoming dance with me Saturday night?"

Kara felt warm under Todd's gaze. She giggled. "I don't know, Todd. I'm not sure if I can trust you."

"Trust me? What's that supposed to mean?"

Blushing, Kara looked away. "I like you, Todd. I like you a lot. Now that you share my faith, you are even more special to me."

Todd squeezed her hand, pretending to pout. "So, what's the problem?"

"The problem is," Kara said as pink crept into her cheeks, "I'm not so sure that I'm ready to be alone with you."

Todd patted her hand. "I promise not to bite."

Kara giggled again. "It's not your bite I'm worried about. It's your kisses."

Todd grinned. "How about if we double-date? Would that help you feel better?"

"That's a great idea. But who could we go with?"

"Jack and Brooke?"

Shaking her head, Kara said, "No way!"

"Well, then, how about Dee Ann and Matt?"

"I'm . . . I'm sot so sure that's a good idea," Kara confessed.

"With the Homecoming court and all, I'm not sure what state Dee Ann will be in."

"Are you kidding? Dee Ann is the kind of girl who's always dreamed of being a Homecoming queen. Almost everyone I know is voting for her. Matt and Queen Dee should be a lot of fun."

"I'll ask her," Kara said. "In the meantime, I hear that Jenni and Ryan Stephens are planning to go."

Todd nodded. "Yeah, I guess they'd be okay to double with. Could you check into it?"

"Sure," Kara said, feeling the warmth of Todd's hand tingle through her fingers. "I'll ask."

Kara looked thoughtful. "Maybe we could all go, you know, like a group date."

"That might be fun," Todd said. "Why don't you see if everyone can come to Eatza My Pizza tonight so we can plan our evening."

"That's a great idea," Kara agreed. "I'll call the gang after school today."

Lord, give me wisdom and lead me away from temptation. Help me not to wink at it but to turn my back on it. Give me creative solutions to the problems that tempt me to stray away from the purity You want for my life.

Additional Scripture reading: Proverbs 4:5–9

❖

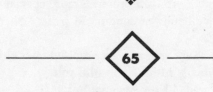

THE PLEDGE
—

**If any of you lacks wisdom, let him ask of God,
who gives to all liberally and without reproach,
and it will be given to him.—James 1:5**

Kara and Jenni walked to the pizzeria early so they would have a chance to chat.

As they sat in a booth, sipping their sodas, Kara asked, "So what did you say when Ryan asked you to the dance?"

Jenni giggled. "Yes, of course."

"I thought you weren't that crazy about Ryan."

"Oh, that was before I got to know him," Jenni confessed. "He's got the deepest brown eyes. Have you ever noticed?"

Kara giggled again. "Well, I've always thought he was cute."

Jenni frowned. "Still, I'm worried. I never know what to say when I'm with him."

Kara nodded. "You don't need to entertain him with a speech. Just ask him questions like, 'What did it feel like to make that winning touchdown?' The next thing you know, you'll be having a real conversation!"

"That should be easy enough," Jenni agreed. "Do you know if Dee Ann told Matt her news yet?"

Kara shook her head as Matt leaned over the top of the booth. "What news?" he asked.

Kara and Jenni froze. "Uh, that she's a shoo-in for Homecoming queen," Kara said, rolling her eyes at Jenni.

"I already knew that!" Matt said, sliding into the booth with the girls.

Soon, all six teens were seated around a huge bubbly hamburger, olive, and onion pizza.

"So, what's the plan?" Ryan asked as he put his arm around Jenni.

Todd answered, "The plan is to go on a group date." He winked at Kara. "You know, to keep everyone out of trouble."

Matt sipped his soda. "That's really a great idea." He smiled at Dee Ann. "Not that we need a chaperone."

Dee Ann fidgeted with her straw. "What exactly is a group date?"

Kara answered, "Well, we'll probably travel together—"

"No, you and Todd can ride with us," Ryan said. "There's no way all of us can fit in one car."

"True," Matt agreed. "Well, then, Dee Ann and I will be right behind you."

"Is that it?" Dee Ann asked, her voice hopeful.

"No," Kara answered, "we'll sit together at the dance."

Ryan said, "But we're only going to stay at the dance for a little while, long enough to show off the new queen." He smiled at Dee Ann. "Then we're going over to the church's alternative party, right?"

"Right," Todd agreed.

"So that's all there is to it?" Dee Ann asked.

Matt asked, "Why don't we go a step further? Why don't we be accountable to each other about our extracurricular activities?"

Jenni looked puzzled. "What do you mean?"

"Let's agree," Matt continued, "not to drink, smoke, do drugs, or take advantage of our dates."

"That sounds like a challenge," Ryan said, stealing a smile from Jenni. "What do you think, Todd?"

Todd winked at Kara. "Well, I can't say that I've ever partied without a beer. But if I can steal a kiss from Kara at her doorstep, I'll consider it."

Kara blushed as Matt said, "Good, then it's agreed." Matt reached for Dee Ann's hand. "This will be the night of our lives. A night to remember."

Lord, I need Your wisdom! Forgive me for sometimes feeling shy around others. Teach me how to take an active interest in my friends and not feel that I have to be the center of attention. I dedicate my friendships to You.

Additional Scripture reading: Ephesians 5:1–12

❖

CAN'T YOU CHANGE YOUR MIND?

Children, obey your parents in the Lord, for
this is right.—Ephesians 6:1

Kara sat in the living room with her parents.

"Anyway, Mom, do you think you and I can go shopping for my Homecoming dress tomorrow?"

Her mom laughed. "I don't see why not, as long as you promise to stay within our budget."

"You can count on me," Kara said with a smile.

Her mom asked, "So the six of you are going out together? What are your plans?"

Kara started, "Well, after Dee Ann is crowned Homecoming queen . . ."

"You're pretty sure about that, are you?" her dad teased.

Kara laughed. "Of course, Dad. Everyone is voting for her. She and the other candidates asked me to be part of their court. I get to smile for the yearbook picture and hold the crown."

Mrs. Daniels looked concerned. "Uh, how is Dee Ann handling all of this?"

"Fine, I think, although she does seem a little nervous," Kara confessed.

"So after you help crown Dee Ann queen, then what?" her father asked.

"Then we're all going over to the Homecoming dance to show Dee Ann off for a little while. After that, we're heading to the church's alternative Homecoming party."

"Who's driving?" her dad asked.

"Todd and I are riding with Jenni and Ryan," Kara answered.

Mr. Daniels looked concerned. "Kara, I don't know why, but that bothers me. It's almost as if I feel that God is telling me it's wrong."

"What do you mean?" Kara asked.

"I don't know for sure, but somehow I know that you should ride with Matt and Dee Ann!"

"Matt and Dee Ann!" Kara wailed. "Dad, I just can't! I don't want to be a little sister tagalong!"

Kara appealed to her mother, "Mom, you understand, don't you? Matt and Dee Ann need a little privacy, right?"

"That's probably true," Mrs. Daniels admitted. "But I have to stand with your father. Whenever he feels he's hearing from God, I've discovered it's a good idea to listen."

"But, Mom!"

Mr. Daniels interrupted, "I'm sorry, Kara. But I'll go this far. I'll explain it to Matt. He'll understand."

Kara's lower lip protruded slightly. "Maybe, but I'm not so sure that Dee Ann, Jenni, Ryan, or Todd will. Can't you change your mind?"

"I'm sorry, Kara, not this time."

"All right, Dad, but my friends will never understand," Kara said, hanging her head.

Mr. Daniels put his arm around his daughter. "I know. But you've got to trust me on this, okay?"

Sighing deeply, Kara answered, "All right."

"Good, now, about that dress. Just how much are you and your mother planning to spend?"

Lord, sometimes it's hard to obey my parents. But teach me how to honor them. Although I know my parents aren't perfect, I know they love me and care for me. Show me how to love and care for them as well.

Additional Scripture reading: Ephesians 6:1–4

❖

HOMECOMING COURT

There is a way that seems right
  to a man,
But its end is the way of
  death.—Proverbs 14:12

Just before halftime, Kara, Brooke, and Dee Ann hurried to change from their cheerleading sweaters and skirts into their Homecoming dresses.

As Kara slipped into her purple satin dress that smoothed around her figure, she called over the partition, "This is so exciting!"

When Dee Ann didn't respond, Brooke said, "I agree, Kara. Wearing the Homecoming crown will be the most exciting moment of my life."

Kara stepped out of the changing room. She couldn't help admiring Brooke's outfit, which consisted of a flirty metallic black-and-gold miniskirt with a matching gold camisole. The ripples of Brooke's dark hair touched the top of her wide patent leather belt.

Kara asked, "Brooke, do you really think you're going to win?"

"Of course! I've made all the right choices. I've ensured my success!" Brooke said as her dangling gold earrings glimmered in the fluorescent light. "Unlike some of the other contestants."

A partition door creaked and Kara turned to admire Dee Ann as she emerged from her dressing room. She was wearing a not-too-tight black organza dress with a fluted hem. Her white three-tiered chiffon collar hung like fluttering wings over her shoulders while her sheer chiffon sleeves highlighted her slender arms. Kara whistled, watching Dee Ann's golden hair sparkle in waves that dramatically flowed over one shoulder.

Kara said, "Dee, you really look beautiful tonight!"

Dee Ann turned to Brooke, ignoring Kara's compliment. "You're probably right, Brooke," Dee Ann said in a monotone whisper. "Our paths have taken a different twist."

Kara freshened her makeup, pondering Dee Ann's remark. Suddenly, it was time for the girls to rush to their places on the sidelines. They arrived just in time to watch the end of the last play of the second quarter. When the clock ran out, the football players trotted by, heading for their locker room. As the players passed, Todd and Ryan called in unison, "Go for it, Dee! We believe in you!"

When the band started, the girls walked to their places on the wooden platform that had been pulled onto the field. Kara's knees shook as she held the crown on a blue satin pillow. Mr. Smith tore open the envelope and announced, "And the newest Summitview High Homecoming queen is . . . Miss Brooke Kelly."

The normally boisterous crowd quieted and applauded politely as Mr. Smith placed the rhinestone-studded tiara on Brooke's head.

What happened? Kara wondered. *I don't know anyone who voted for Brooke. Something doesn't seem right.*

She stole a peek at Dee Ann. Dee Ann's hand was half raised in a wave, a smile frozen on her face.

Kara tried to hide a frown. *What's going on?*

Sometimes life doesn't seem fair. But even so, help me realize You can make justice out of injustice and You can lift the oppressed to a place of honor, even when they've been dishonored by the world. For when we honor You, You will go before us, showing us the way to Your heart.

Additional Scripture reading: Psalm 17:1–15

❖

ANGRY HEART

Do not envy the oppressor,
And choose none of his ways.
—Proverbs 3:31

Brooke walked to a waiting red convertible for her victory ride around the field. As Brooke waved at her mostly silent classmates, Kara and Dee Ann scurried to the girls' locker room to change into their cheerleading uniforms.

"I'm sorry, Dee," Kara said. "I was so sure you'd win."

Dee Ann's face turned to stone, and her eyes flashed with anger. "Kara, the vote was rigged."

Kara whirled to face Dee Ann. "What?"

Dee Ann swiped at a tear that had dared to escape her scowl. "Last Saturday, who do you think drove me to the clinic?"

"I don't know. I thought you took the bus."

Dee Ann shook her head. "No. Coach Lovett drove us. She was the one who counseled us to get abortions."

"Us? You and who else?" Kara asked.

Dee Ann stared at the wall. "The coach made it clear. Summitview High would not honor a pregnant teen with the Homecoming crown. Even though I won the popular vote, the school withheld my crown anyway. So you see, I lost the contest the night I lost my virginity."

Kara tried to put her arm around Dee Ann, but Dee Ann stiffened. Drawing back, Kara studied Dee Ann's smoldering eyes.

"I hate him," Dee Ann whispered, her voice cracking with anger.

"Who? Jack?"

Dee Ann raised her voice, "I hate him."

Kara scanned the locker room. "Dee, someone might hear you."

Jerking her head, Dee Ann glared at Kara. "I don't care. I hope everyone knows. I hate Jack so much I wish he were dead!"

Stepping back, Kara said, "Dee, don't talk like that. Sure, Jack's a jerk. He hurt you. But you can't let hatred rule your life. You've got to let go."

"Never!" Dee Ann blurted, "Never! I'll hate Jack forever!"

Dee Ann's face twisted with rage. "Don't you see, Kara?" she pleaded. "Because of what Jack did to me, my dreams are dead. Soon, I'll be the most whispered about girl on campus. I've lost the crown, my reputation, the cheerleading squad . . ."

"The squad?"

"By the orders of the coach," Dee Ann said. "Jenni's in. I'm out."

"I'm sorry."

"Well, you can't expect a pregnant girl to bounce around with pom-poms. It's bad for the school's image."

"It isn't fair, is it?" Kara asked. "You were the one who did the right thing by not having an abortion. You saved a life. It seems to me that they should make you a hero."

Dee Ann shook her head, allowing her rage to hide behind a plastic mask. She asked, "What do you think Matt will say?"

"I don't know," Kara admitted. "But he'll probably want to punch Jack's lights out."

"What do you think he'll think about me?"

Kara shook her head. "When are you going to tell him?"

"I don't know. I thought I'd tell him tonight. And I will if it seems right. If not, I guess I'll tell him after church tomorrow."

"I'll be praying for you," Kara said.

I'm starting to figure this out. Lord, You don't want us to forgive others because it's the fair thing to do. You want us to forgive others, regardless of fairness. For when our spirits are full of hate, we stop growing in You. In fact, we actually shrink. Help me forgive my enemies, even when I have no reason other than obedience and love for You.

Additional Scripture reading: Proverbs 3:31–35

❖

GLOATERS

For You will save the humble people,
But will bring down haughty looks.
—Psalm 18:27

After Dee Ann's explanation of the rigged contest, Kara's cheers felt hollow.

When the football game was over, Kara slipped back into her shimmering dress and met her friends in the parking lot.

Todd greeted her with a warm smile. "You look beautiful, Kara."

"Where's Dee?" Matt asked.

"She'll be here in a minute," Kara said.

Shaking his head, Matt said, "I still can't believe that Dee Ann lost to Brooke."

Todd nodded in agreement. "It's weird, you know. The whole

football team was baffled, that is, all except Jack. He was bragging to anyone who would listen."

"Don't say anything to Dee Ann about her loss," Kara said. "She's trying to be brave, but I think she feels like crying."

The group collectively held their breath as Dee Ann scurried toward them. "Sorry for the holdup," she apologized.

Matt squeezed her hand. "Don't worry about it, Dee. You're worth the wait."

Blushing, Dee Ann said, "So, is everyone ready to go?"

Before anyone could respond, Jack and Brooke elbowed their way into the circle.

Jack faced Matt. "My condolences, Pard. It's too bad you got stuck with a loser! But, then, I guess not everyone's got the stuff to keep a queen happy."

Matt glared at Jack. "Dee Ann will always be a queen in my book."

Jack sneered, "Is that so? I wonder—"

Dee Ann interrupted. "You must be thrilled, Brooke. Congratulations."

Brooke responded with a triumphant smile. She said, "I am, Dee. You don't know what you're missing."

Kara said, "Uh, are you two going to the dance?"

"Of course, as soon as I get another couple of six-packs," Jack answered.

Todd observed, "Jack, you were already hitting the bottle pretty hard in the locker room. Are you sure you need more?"

Laughing, Jack pulled Brooke toward his truck. "Of course, Todd. It's the only way to party! But I don't have to tell you!"

As Jack peeled out of the parking lot, Kara faced Todd. "What did Jack mean? Have you been drinking, too?"

Todd shook his head. "Jack's referring to my recent past." He grinned at her. "I made a pact with the gang, remember?"

"I'm sorry to suspect you, Todd. It's just that Jack puts me on edge," Kara said.

Ryan laughed. "Kara, I think that goes for all of us."

"Well, what are we waiting for? Shall we walk to the gym?" Jenni asked.

Matt said, "Let's keep our visit to the dance short. Jack seems to be looking for trouble, and I don't want him to find it at the end of my fist."

The group laughed. Kara said, "Sure thing. We'll just stay long enough to show everyone that we're not sore losers. Right, Dee Ann?"

Thank You for changing my life. I know that if I had stayed on the course I had planned for myself, I would be lost. Thanks for finding me and giving me a map that keeps me in Your unconditional love. Help me stay on track, avoiding wrong turns that would lead me to trouble.

Additional Scripture reading: Psalm 31:19–24

❖

THE FIGHT

But You, O LORD, are a shield for
  me,
My glory and the One who lifts up
  my head.—Psalm 3:3

Applause greeted Kara and her friends when they arrived at the dance. Terrald Grant, one of the guys on the football team, shouted, "We love you, Dee Ann!"

Grinning, Dee Ann waved back. Laura Winsor, one of the other cheerleaders, raced to meet her. "Dee, none of us can figure out why you didn't win. Everyone voted for you!"

Beaming, Matt said, "That's what I told her. It was obviously some sort of mistake."

Dee Ann shook her head. "On my part."

"What?" Laura asked. "How can you say that? Obviously, some-one miscounted the votes!"

Shrugging, Dee Ann said, "It's okay. Brooke made a beautiful queen."

Laura fluffed her newly permed hair. "Brooke was almost impos-sible to live with before she was crowned queen. Think how con-ceited she'll be now!"

Terrald joined Laura. "As far as I'm concerned, you're the *real* Homecoming queen!"

He turned around and yelled, "Let's cheer for Dee. She's queen, regardless of who's wearing the crown!"

The crowd stamped and yelled as Dee Ann brushed away a tear. Kara hugged her. "See, the kids know which candidate got the most votes. Maybe they shouldn't call attention to it, but they know the contest wasn't fair."

Suddenly, the cheering stopped. Kara and her friends turned around to see Jack and Brooke standing in the gymnasium door.

Jack charged toward Dee Ann, pulling Brooke behind him. Brooke stumbled to keep up, holding her lopsided crown on her head.

"What do you think you're doing?" Jack shouted. "Brooke's the queen, not you, you little cow!"

Matt stepped between Dee Ann and Jack. "I'm sorry you wit-nessed this scene. But you can't talk to my date like that!"

"Your date is a piece of trash," Jack blurted.

Kara tugged on Matt's arm. "Maybe it's time to leave," she said as two adult chaperones sprinted toward them.

Matt continued to glare at Jack. "That's not a bad idea. I smell a real stinker."

Drawing his arm back, Jack readied to take a swing. "I'll teach you!" he roared.

Matt sidestepped the blow, and Jack stumbled to the floor.

The crowd cheered for Matt as Jack pulled himself up. Jack growled, "Why, you!" He hurled his body at Matt, who sidestepped him again.

"Jack, you're drunk! Too drunk to fight!"

Matt turned to join his friends waiting for him at the door, and Jack tackled him from behind. Matt thudded to the floor, and Jack hammered his fist into the back of Matt's head.

Scrambling to his feet, Matt seethed, "Jack, you asked for it!" He smacked his fist into Jack's stomach. Jack doubled in pain, and Matt waved to the stunned crowd. "Sorry to stop the show, but beating up drunks just isn't my style."

Jack fell to the floor, and Matt and his friends headed for the parking lot, slamming the gym door behind them. Slowly, Jack wobbled to his feet, screaming to their unhearing ears, "I'll get you for this! We'll settle this tonight!"

The world brings trouble, but You bring blessings. Give me the power to share Your blessings with others. Teach me how to lead my friends out of the world's pain and into Your loving embrace.

Additional Scripture reading: Psalm 140:1–4

❖

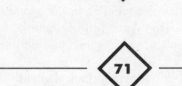

THE CRASH

Make no friendship with an angry man,
And with a furious man do not go,
Lest you learn his ways
And set a snare for your soul.
—Proverbs 22:24–25

Jenni and Ryan scurried to their car while Kara, Todd, Matt, and Dee Ann hurried to theirs. Matt started the engine. "Dee, I'm sorry for that scene."

Dee Ann patted his arm. "It's okay, Matt, really. I'm glad you didn't get hurt. Did you?"

Chuckling, Matt said, "He crowned me pretty good, but I'm okay."

"Speaking of crowns," Kara said, "how did you like the way the kids rallied around Dee Ann?"

"It was great! Dee, how did it feel?" Todd asked.

Matt pulled onto the street, making a right turn.

Dee Ann hesitated. "It meant a lot," she said as a shy smile lit her face.

Kara giggled, turning to see if Jenni and Ryan were following in their car. Her giggle turned into a gasp.

Matt looked in his rearview mirror. "What's wrong, Kara?"

"It's Jack and Brooke. I hope they're not planning to chase us!"

"Maybe I'd better head toward the police station," Matt said, gunning his motor. "Car chases are risky. Someone could get hurt!"

To Kara's horror, she watched Jack climb behind the wheel of his truck as Brooke scooted next to him. Jack roared his engine, lunging his truck toward the exit just as Ryan and Jenni pulled into the street. Jack's truck raced with power, swerving to avoid hitting another car that was pulling into the lot. Out of control, Jack's truck barreled over the curb, plowing into Ryan's car.

The crunch of metal twisting against metal shattered the darkness.

"Oh, no!" Kara cried.

"What's happening?" Dee Ann asked, straining to see.

Kara screamed, "Stop the car! He's rammed into Jenni and Ryan!"

Matt pulled over to the side of the road, and Kara scrambled out. Running down the street, Kara could see Jenni's body crumpled in a heap in the middle of the road.

"JENNI!" she screamed. "Weren't you wearing your seatbelt?"

Reaching Jenni's body, Kara knelt, sobbing.

Blood flowed into Jenni's face. Her eyes fluttered open. "Where am I?"

"Try not to talk," Kara said, choking back a cry.

Jenni mumbled groggily, "Everything's so dark."

Grabbing Jenni's hand, Kara encouraged, "Hang in there, Jenni. Okay?"

Jenni shut her eyes and whispered, "It's funny, Kara. Not so long ago, I wanted to die. But now my life has changed. I want to live. Please, God, let me live."

Help me avoid close friendships with angry people. And if anger rules my heart, I turn it over to You. Help me take advantage of every opportunity to share Your love with others.

Additional Scripture reading: Proverbs 23:17–21

❖

BROOKE'S CONFESSION

Can a woman forget her nursing child,
And not have compassion on the son of
    her womb?
Surely they may forget,
Yet I will not forget you.—Isaiah 49:15

A car squealed to a halt, and a woman rushed to Kara's side. "I'm a nurse," she shouted, pulling Kara back. "Give your friend some air!"

Kara stood up, backing into Todd's gentle grasp. Todd said, "Kara, are you okay?"

Kara shook her head.

"Somebody help me," a voice cried from the direction of Jack's truck.

Kara and Todd hurried toward the call.

When they peered into the window, they could see Jack was out cold, crumpled against his steering wheel. The passenger door was ajar, and Brooke was sprawled onto the pavement, her neck twisted at an odd angle. "Help me," she moaned.

Dee Ann was already by her side.

Brooke tried to shift her twisted body. "I . . . I can't move!"

Dee Ann stroked Brooke's luxurious hair as Matt joined them. "Are you in any pain?" Dee Ann asked.

"I . . . I can't feel anything," Brooke confessed.

"Don't try to move her," Matt warned, "her neck might be broken."

"This is what I deserve, Dee. This is what I deserve for killing my baby," Brooke moaned.

"Shhh, don't talk about that," Dee Ann whispered.

"I . . . I didn't have the courage to walk out," Brooke gasped. "Not like you did. The crown wasn't worth it. My baby's dead. But your baby . . . your baby has life!"

Kara shot a look at Matt before kneeling beside Brooke. "Dee Ann's right. You mustn't talk about that." She patted Brooke's hand. "Besides, what happened is past. God doesn't try to get even with us. God will forgive you if you ask Him. He's holding your baby in His arms."

Brooke smiled weakly. "Then maybe I can join them."

The whine of a siren drowned her words as a paramedic rushed to Brooke's side.

"Step back everyone," she said.

Kara and Dee Ann stood up, and Matt asked, "Where are you taking them?"

"To Summitview General if they make it," the paramedic replied.

Kara stood just in time to see Ryan stagger from his car. "Ryan!" she called, running to give him a hug. "Are you okay?"

Looking confused, Ryan said, "I . . . I think so. Where's Jenni?"

Kara pointed with her head to the paramedics who were hoisting Jenni onto a stretcher. Ryan stumbled to her side. "Jenni!"

Kara turned to Dee Ann. "This has got to be a bad dream. I can't believe this is happening!"

Dee Ann nodded. "Brooke's right," she whispered. "The crown wasn't worth it."

Nodding in silent agreement, Kara thought, *I hope Matt agrees.*

Lord, there is nothing You can't forgive. But even in Your forgiveness, there is often a price the world forces us to pay. Help me live my life in such a way that my regrets will be few and my life will be whole. Thank You for forgetting my sins while remembering me with Your love.

Additional Scripture reading: Romans 3:23–27

❖

WHERE'S GOD?

Let us therefore come boldly to the throne of grace, that we may obtain mercy and find grace to help in time of need.—Hebrews 4:16

Matt drove behind the screaming ambulances. Todd whispered, "Why did this happen? Where was God?"

Kara reached for his hand. "God's not responsible for the actions of people like Jack."

"But," Todd argued, "couldn't God have prevented this?"

Grimacing, Matt said, "He could have. But He lets us be responsible for our own actions. Jack chose to drink and drive. This is a consequence."

"I guess a few weeks ago, when I was still drinking, the same thing could have happened to me," Todd mused.

Kara nodded. Todd continued, "But what I want to know is, where is God now? Can He pick up the pieces? Can He put Jack, Jenni, and Brooke back together?"

Kara said, "We need to pray."

"I don't know how to pray," Todd confessed. "What should I say?"

Matt gripped the steering wheel hard. "Pray for God's mercy and healing power."

"Yes," Kara agreed. "In the name of Jesus."

"Will God heal them?" Todd asked.

"I hope so. I know He's listening."

"Jesus healed the sick," Todd said. "Didn't He say that if we had enough faith, we could do the same?"

"Yes, He did," Kara answered. "But be careful that you don't put faith in your own faith. That doesn't work. Put your faith in God. Seek His face and trust Him with the results, even if it means . . ."

"Even if it means someone dies?"

Kara nodded. "Well, dying is not always the worst thing that could happen to a person. But, of course, we do need to bind the Enemy."

Todd questioned, "Bind the Enemy?"

"I mean we need to ask God to remove Satan's hand and control from this situation, in Jesus' name," Kara answered. "Then, we've battled. We've done all we can do. The rest is up to God."

"But the kids could die?" Todd asked.

"I'm not sure. Jenni's body might die, but her soul can't. She knows God."

"But what about Brooke?" Dee Ann asked.

"I'm ashamed to say," Kara answered, "I don't know if Brooke knows God or not. I've never asked."

The group fell silent.

Todd said, "Kara, do you mind if I pray out loud?"

"Please do."

Bowing his head, Todd prayed, "Lord, I'm just getting to know You, and I need Your help. I bind Satan from this situation in Jesus' name. I pray that You will have mercy on Brooke, Jenni, and Jack. Give them Your healing power. Don't let them die. Let them live!"

Kara whispered, "In Jesus' name."

Todd echoed, "In Jesus' name. Amen."

Show me how to pray and show me how to trust You. Help me not to be fooled into thinking I can control You. Rather, comfort me by reminding me that You turn bad situations into good situations. Grow my faith and help me not to rely on my own under-

standing. Thank You that I can boldly come to Your throne with this request.

Additional Scripture reading: Romans 8:26–28

❖

THE
DISCOVERY

**For the Holy Spirit will teach you in that very
hour what you ought to say.—Luke 12:12**

When the kids arrived at the hospital, they were ushered into a waiting room.

As the hours ticked by, the group sat praying silently.

Finally, Todd left to see if he could find some answers.

When he returned, his face was clouded with worry.

Matt asked, "What did you find out?"

"Not much," Todd admitted. "Jack and Jenni are still unconscious, and Brooke's in surgery. Ryan appears to be okay, but they're holding him for observation."

Kara asked, "When will they know something?"

"Probably not until morning," Todd responded. "I've called my mom to come and pick me up. I'll come back tomorrow."

As Todd headed for the front door, Matt turned to Dee Ann.

"Dee, something Brooke said has been troubling me."

Kara's eyebrows shot off an alarm. "Guys, I think I'll look for a water fountain."

"No," Dee Ann said, "stay. I need you."

Kara stared at her hands.

Matt tried again. "Just what did Brooke mean when she said that her baby was dead, but your baby has life?"

Dee Ann reached for Matt's hand. "Matt, there's something I've been needing to tell you. I guess this is as good a time as any."

"Tell me what, Dee?" Matt asked, his brows knitting together. "I know you can't be pregnant, you and I haven't . . ."

Dee Ann slumped her shoulders, then tentatively sought Matt's eyes. "But I am, Matt."

"But . . . but that's impossible!"

"I'm pregnant with Jack's baby."

Matt bolted out of his chair. His voice thundered through the waiting room, "WHAT?"

"Sit down, Matt," Dee Ann pleaded. "I want to explain."

Slowly, Matt sat in his chair. "Are you telling me that you and Jack . . . ?"

"It's not what you think."

"Not what I think? I know enough about biology to know what had to have happened!"

Matt started to rise. Kara said, "Wait, Matt. Listen to what Dee has to say."

Whirling in anger, Matt faced Kara. "What? You're in on this?"

Kara patted the seat of Matt's chair. "This has been a long night. Sit down and shut up. Hear Dee Ann out."

Matt sat again. "All right, I'm listening." He folded his arms. "This better be good because my reputation has just gone down the tubes."

Bristling, Kara said, "Mom and I think that the trauma of a stained reputation pales in light of the trauma Dee Ann's lived through."

"Mom? You mean Mom knows, too?" Matt fumed. "Am I the last person in the world to find out? What's going on here?"

Sometimes, telling the truth hurts. But that's what You would have me do. Help me to be honest, but at the same time, give me wisdom and tact. Teach me what I ought to say. Help me not to hide from the truth but to take shelter in it.

Additional Scripture reading: Ephesians 3:16–21

❖

THE
EXPLANATION

—

There is therefore now no condemnation to those who are in Christ Jesus.—Romans 8:1

"I'll tell you what happened," Dee Ann said to Matt as she tried to hide behind her hair.

He folded his arms. "I'm listening."

Blushing, Dee Ann said, "This all started in our social studies class . . . when I didn't take a stand against premarital sex. Jack must have thought I was an easy mark.

"I knew what he expected when he asked me out. But I figured I'd just tell him no.

"That's when I made another mistake and got drunk. I didn't realize what an overpowering effect alcohol would have on me. I couldn't think straight. I tried to stop Jack's advances, but he wouldn't take no for an answer."

Matt refolded his arms.

"I guess I should have gone to the police," Dee Ann said. "I've been told that the rape trauma team at the hospital could have tried to help me prevent this pregnancy. But I felt guilty and dirty. I wanted to hide my shame from the world."

Dee Ann's eyes glistened. "But it wouldn't stay hidden. When I suspected I was pregnant, I went to Coach Lovett. She took Brooke and me to the Summitview Women's Clinic."

"Brooke?" Matt asked. "She's pregnant, too?"

"She was," Dee Ann said. "You see, after my incident with Jack, he picked up with Brooke."

Matt looked skeptical. "Did Jack rape Brooke, too?"

"I don't think so."

"So, you're telling me that both you and Brooke ended up pregnant by Jack?"

"That's right," Dee Ann said, shielding her eyes with her hands. "When the positive pregnancy results were in, we had a chat with Coach Lovett. The coach said abortion was the only way out, that is, if we wanted to stay on the cheerleading squad and run for Homecoming queen. At first, I believed her. I even went so far as to schedule an abortion, along with Brooke. But as it turned out, I couldn't go through with it.

"That's when I ran into Kara and your mom at the clinic.

"I knew what keeping my baby would mean. I would lose my slot on the squad, my chance for being Homecoming queen. But the worst part was, I would lose you."

Matt stared at the floor.

"I have lost you, haven't I?"

Matt stood up. "This is too much for me, Dee. If all that you said is true, I'm truly sorry for you. But I don't think I can deal with it."

Hanging her head, Dee Ann said, "I was afraid you'd feel this way. And I'm sorry. Really sorry."

Dee Ann lifted her head. "My life has fallen apart around me. But I'm glad of one thing,"

"What's that?" Matt asked, trying to rub the disbelief from his eyes.

"What Brooke said was true. The Homecoming crown was not worth the price of killing our babies. I know I didn't ask for this pregnancy, but it's not right to stop it. This baby is going to live. He's going to have a hope and a future."

*Thank You for not condemning life, no matter how it starts—
even the lives of the unborn. I realize some people think unborn
babies are nothing more than clumps of cells, but when you get
right down to it, that's all I am, too. Thank You for creating the*

wonderful mystery of hidden life in the womb. Help it become a safe place for our nation's children.

Additional Scripture reading: Psalm 139:13–16

THE
CHALLENGE

For with God nothing will be impossible.
—Luke 1:37

Dee Ann looked into Matt's eyes. "I'm sorry. I never meant to hurt you."

Matt looked down at her and whispered, "Then why do I feel betrayed?"

Dee Ann looked away. "I wouldn't blame you if you never forgave me. I'll understand. As for me, I'll never forgive Jack. Not only has he ruined my life, he's ruined the lives of my friends."

"Excuse me. I don't mean to interrupt, but I couldn't help over-hearing some of what you said," a male voice said from behind.

The teens started, turning to face their eavesdropper.

Kara exclaimed, "Pastor Jeff! How long have you been standing there?"

"Long enough to know what's going on," Jeff Hoffman, the youth director, admitted.

Matt stood up. "I'd like to stay and chat. But I need some fresh air. I think I'll go for a little walk. I've got a lot of thinking to do."

Dee Ann drooped as Matt stalked out the door. Jeff sat down in Matt's chair and put his arm around Dee Ann's shoulder. "Are you okay?"

Dee Ann shook her head, afraid to release her surging emotions. Withdrawing his arm, Jeff addressed Kara. "I heard what happened. I got here as soon as I could. How are the kids doing?"

Kara bit her lip. She said, "Ryan's going to be okay. Jack's still unconscious, Brooke's in surgery, and Jenni . . ." She blinked hard. "Jenni's still in a coma. The extent of her injuries is unknown."

Dee Ann sniffled and Jeff handed her his hanky. As she wiped her eyes, Jeff said, "Dee Ann, I realize you've been through a lot. And I admire you for saving the life of your baby, but there's something you said that frightened me."

Dee Ann looked up. "What?"

"Do you really hate Jack Raymond?"

Dee Ann studied her fingernails and nodded.

Jeff said, "In light of what's happened, you certainly have the right. But that's beside the point."

Cocking her head, Dee Ann asked, "What do you mean?"

"Regardless of our rights, we still need to forgive."

"Kara's already given me that lecture," Dee Ann admitted. "But I'm stuck. Even if I wanted to forgive Jack, which I don't, I can't imagine having the power to do it. Don't you realize what he's done? He raped me. He got Brooke pregnant. He hurt and maybe even killed my friends."

Jeff nodded. "That's not the issue."

"How can you say that?"

"God wants you to forgive Jack not just for Jack's sake but for *your* sake."

"But I can't. It's not in my heart."

"That's okay."

"Okay?"

"It's almost impossible for us to forgive in our own power, and when the offense is as big as Jack's, the idea of forgiving seems absurd. But it's still possible."

"How?"

"First of all, you need to see that your hatred of Jack is like a cancer to your spirit. You have to ask yourself, Is my grudge worth my own spiritual death?"

Jeff studied Dee Ann hard as she lowered her eyes. "If you decide it isn't, you need to pray something like, 'God, although I don't feel like forgiving Jack, I choose to forgive him anyway because

I love You. Give me the power and strength to forgive. Free me from hate.'"

Jeff confessed, "There will be times you'll stumble in your decision but continue to seek God's power. He won't let you down."

Dee Ann stared at Jeff blankly.

Jeff asked, "So what do you say? Would you be willing to consider forgiving Jack?"

"Maybe. I'll have to think about it."

Jeff gave her a hug. "Good. That's a step in the right direction. Now, do you girls need a ride home?"

Give me the power to forgive my enemies, and help me overcome hate. Instead, replace my hurt with the power of Your love. Show me how to love others, no matter the cost. I know that with You, nothing is impossible.

Additional Scripture reading: Hebrews 12:14–15

TRUE FAITH

It shall come to pass
That before they call, I will answer;
And while they are still speaking, I
will hear.—Isaiah 65:24

Kara spent the night tossing and turning with prayers. "Don't let Jenni die! Help Brooke," she'd cried in her dreams. As the moon hid behind a cloud, Kara woke with a start. *Help Jenni,* she pleaded, closing her eyes again. *Don't let her die!*

Suddenly, dawn seemed to glow into Kara's room. She peeked out. *Is it time to get up? No, the clock reads four o'clock.*

Pulling her covers higher, Kara wondered, *What's happening?*

She felt herself being wrapped in a blanket of love, and her mind heard a voice her ears couldn't hear. "Jenni will be all right."

Is that You, Lord? Kara prayed.

The presence of His love grew stronger.

Lord, what about Brooke?

"Trust Me," the voice replied as His presence faded.

The next morning, when the alarm went off, Kara thought about her experience. *Was it a dream?*

No, she decided with a sigh of relief. *It was God. The presence, the love, the message—it had to be.*

When she sat down at the breakfast table, her father asked, "Is that the hint of a smile I see on your face?"

Kara nodded. "A hint," she agreed.

Her mother asked, "You can smile after what happened?"

Reaching for a steaming muffin, Kara responded. "I'm convinced that Jenni's going to be okay."

Her parents exchanged glances. Her dad asked, "How do you know?"

"It's hard to explain, but I guess you can call it faith," Kara answered.

Her mom asked, "Are you sure it's not presumption?"

"Presumption is when we insist that God follow our will instead of finding His will. But as I sought God last night, I felt He told me that Jenni would be okay."

Her dad smiled. "That's great! I'm glad you sought God on this. It was wonderful of Him to answer you."

"Dad, does God always move in this way?"

Shaking his head, he answered, "No, we can't put God in a box unless we have a universe full of boxes. God moves through our hope and faith, and He also moves through His compassion, love, and mercy. He even heals those who don't know His name. At times He seems silent, like He's ignoring our pleas for help. That's when we need to trust Him most. When we do, God will always turn the situation into good."

Kara's mom interrupted, "Do you feel God spoke to you about Brooke?"

"I'm a little confused," Kara admitted. "He did, but . . ."

"But what?" her mom asked.

"He said to trust Him. Do you think that means He's going to heal her?"

"I'm not sure," her dad answered. "Maybe. Maybe not."

Kara nodded. "I was afraid you would say that."

Mr. Daniels said, "It's exciting when God speaks to us. This reminds me of when God prompted me to forbid you to ride in Ryan's car. It didn't make sense at the time, but it does now. Kara, I'm so glad you honored my instructions."

"Me, too." Kara looked at the kitchen door. "Isn't Matt coming down to breakfast?"

"He's still in his room," her mom said. "Bryce should be down any minute, but Matt said he didn't feel like eating."

"I'm not surprised," Kara said. "He took Dee Ann's news pretty hard. I think he feels like our whole family betrayed him. I hope he can forgive us."

Thank You for being real. You're not a figment of my imagination. You are the awesome, living God. Thank You for caring enough about me to hear my prayers. Thank You for answering before I call. Thank You for loving me enough to know and care about my needs.

Additional Scripture reading: John 16:7–14

FREE!

And whenever you stand praying, if you have
anything against anyone, forgive him, that your
Father in heaven may also forgive you your
trespasses.—Mark 11:25

Kara tiptoed to the nurses' station in the hallway outside the
Intensive Care Unit. The smell of antiseptic soap stung her nostrils.

When the nurse looked up, Kara asked, "Can you tell me how
Jack Raymond, Ryan Stephens, Jenni Baker, and Brooke Kelly are?"

The nurse crinkled her notes. "Let's see, Jack Raymond. He's
out of ICU. He's in room 201-A." The nurse's bony finger searched
for Ryan's name. "Ryan Stephens, did you say?"

Kara nodded.

"He was released this morning."

"How about Brooke Kelly?"

"Ummm, she got out of surgery about 2:00 A.M. It says here
that she's not allowed any visitors, except for immediate family."

"We're on the same cheerleading squad. Does that count?"

The nurse shook her head. "Not unless you get special permis-
sion."

"How about Jenni Baker?"

"She's still in ICU. Listed in critical condition. The note says,
'absolutely no visitors, except family.' "

Kara's heart sank. *Could I be mistaken about the message from
the Lord? No*, she decided, *I'll continue to believe.*

When Kara got to the waiting room, she was surprised to see Dee
Ann already there. "How's it going?" Kara asked.

Shrugging, Dee Ann answered, "Okay, I guess. I got here early.
Nothing much has happened, except I've had some time to think
about what Jeff said last night. Uh, how's Matt?"

"I'm not sure," Kara admitted. "He was still in his room when Mom drove me over."

The hallway door opened, and Mrs. Raymond, Jack's mother, tentatively entered the waiting room. Her voice was filled with remorse as she asked, "Dee Ann, are you here to see Brooke? What's the word on her condition?"

Kara and Dee exchanged glances. Dee Ann said, "Touch and go, I guess. How's Jack?"

"He's still a little groggy but coherent," Mrs. Raymond said.

"Do you think he's up for company?" Dee Ann asked.

Kara grabbed her arm. "Dee Ann!"

"It's okay, Kara, I've got something I need to tell him."

"I suppose it would be okay," Mrs. Raymond said, "but I must warn you. Jack's in one of his nasty moods."

Mrs. Raymond's heels clicked as she led the girls down the hallway to Jack's door. "I think I'll wait out here," she said.

Kara and Dee Ann stepped into the darkened room. "Jack?" Dee Ann called.

"Well, if it isn't the little troublemaker," Jack said, propping himself up on one elbow.

Dee Ann hesitated. "Jack, I've come to tell you something."

"You're not going to try to pin your illegitimate baby on me, are you?" Jack asked.

Kara shifted uneasily as Dee Ann shook her head, sighing. "No, Jack. It's hard to blame someone who's never responsible for his actions."

"What's that supposed to mean?"

"It means, I give up, Jack. I give up my hate for you, and I give up my resentment of how you've treated me."

"Oh, how noble of you," Jack sneered.

"I realize that my forgiveness means nothing to you," Dee Ann continued, "and that's okay. I'm doing this for myself, for God, and for my baby. Jack, you no longer hold any ties over me. I no longer fear you. I only grieve for you. I'm totally free of you now and forever."

Thank You for providing a way for us to be free through Your forgiveness. And thank You that You provided a way for me to for-

give others. Help me keep myself free of obstacles that would hinder my freedom.

Additional Scripture reading: John 8:31–36

❖

FAITHFUL

God is faithful, by whom you were called into the fellowship of His Son, Jesus Christ our Lord.—1 Corinthians 1:9

Later that afternoon, Kara sat alone in the ICU waiting room, praying for her friends.

Thank You, Jesus, she prayed, *that Jenni's going to be okay, despite how it appears. Please help Brooke. I trust You with her life. I pray that You will turn this situation into good.*

"Kara?"

Mrs. Baker stood in the ICU doorway. "Jenni's coming around. She's asking for you."

Kara jumped out of her seat, following Mrs. Baker to Jenni's partitioned room.

Jenni appeared pale against her sheets. A bandage covered her head.

"Hi, Partner," Kara said. "It's good to see you, but we've got to stop meeting like this."

Smiling groggily, Jenni said, "No kidding."

"So, what's the bandage for?" Kara teased. "Your Halloween costume?"

"I wish," Jenni replied. "Did you know they shaved part of my scalp?"

"Things could be worse," Kara replied.

"I know," Jenni said, creasing her forehead. "Ow, I've got to remember not to do that." She touched her bandage. "So, how's everyone doing?"

"Ryan got to go home this morning," Kara said.

"I know, he dropped by to see me."

"It looks like Jack's going to be okay. I guess he had his seatbelt on. Can you believe it?"

"That figures. Jack'll probably get away with this too, just like he got away with Dee Ann's rape."

"I wouldn't be so sure. His alcohol level was 0.8. That's over the legal limit. He's definitely facing a drunk driving charge, and if he's convicted as an adult, he could face a jail sentence."

"I can't say it wouldn't be what he deserved," Jenni confessed.

"Well, there is another possibility," Kara said.

"What's that?"

"He may be facing a vehicular manslaughter charge."

Jenni gasped. "Someone died?"

"No," Kara explained, "but Brooke is hovering between life and death. The doctors say it could go either way."

"Oh, no!"

Jenni's mother interrupted. "Kara, I think Jenni's starting to tire. Maybe it would be best for you to visit again later."

"Sure, Mrs. Baker," Kara said. "But before I go, I want to say one more thing. No matter what happens to Brooke, just know that God is faithful. We can trust Him."

You are just and faithful. Thank You that I can trust You and not be afraid. You give me hope and show me the way. Help me to always follow Your voice.

Additional Scripture reading: Psalm 12:5–7

❖

LIFE
OR DEATH?

Our soul waits for the LORD;
He is our help and our shield.
For our heart shall rejoice in Him,
Because we have trusted in His holy
name.—Psalm 33:20–21

Sara Penrose appeared at the entrance to the ICU waiting room. She rushed to Kara's side. "I just heard the news. I was headed for another rally, but I thought I'd stop to see how you and Dee Ann are doing."

Kara stood up from her chair and reached for Sara's hand. "Dee Ann's not here right now, but I have a feeling she's going to be fine," Kara said.

"And you?"

"I'm okay. But I am worried about Brooke Kelly."

"The new Homecoming queen?"

Kara looked up to see Mrs. Kelly scurrying toward the double doors that led to the Intensive Care Unit.

"Yes. There's her mom." Kara jumped to her feet and called, "Mrs. Kelly!"

Brooke's mother turned as Kara and Sara joined her. "Kara! How good of you to come by!" Mrs. Kelly eyed Sara, "Are you a friend of Brooke's?"

Before Sara could answer, Kara gushed, "This is Sara, Sara Penrose. How's Brooke doing?"

Mrs. Kelly shook her head. "The doctors think her neck is broken."

A voice called from behind, "Pardon me, Mrs. Kelly?"

The trio turned to see a white-coated doctor quicken his step.

Mrs. Kelly said, "Dr. Drake, are you making your rounds?"

"Yes, I missed you earlier. I'm glad I caught you."

Sighing, Mrs. Kelly said, "It looks bad, doesn't it?"

The doctor nodded.

"Tell me," Mrs. Kelly asked, "what's the chance of Brooke coming out of this thing normal?"

"She's definitely going to have some disabilities. How many, we can't say."

Mrs. Kelly steeled herself. "In that case, I want you to start withholding her fluids and food. That's legal for adults in this state, isn't it? Brooke is eighteen."

Kara darted a look at Sara as the doctor continued, "Yes, but I don't think we should be too hasty. We need to give Brooke some more time. Brooke is alive. The EEG shows brain activity."

Shaking her head, Mrs. Kelly said, "No, I can't stand the thought of my daughter having a disability."

"Well, I'd recommend you think about it another day or two. A week would be even better. In the meantime, Brooke needs all the nourishment she can get."

Mrs. Kelly's eyes glistened. "If you insist, but if Brooke can't be normal, I think she'd rather be dead!"

Sara frowned as the doctor turned to leave. Kara asked Mrs. Kelly, "Could we see Brooke?"

"I suppose so," Mrs. Kelly said. "Follow me."

Kara held her breath when she saw the tubes and monitors fastened to Brooke. She looked like a sleeping Barbie doll in a high-tech horror movie. The walls of Brooke's cubicle were plastered with pictures and memorabilia from her childhood.

Kara and Sara stopped to admire a picture of Brooke swimming with a pair of dolphins.

Mrs. Kelly joined them. "You know, I don't have any regrets about Brooke's life. She was in touch with nature. She communed with dolphins. But now . . . now it looks as if her life is through."

Kara winced and peeked at Brooke out of the corner of her eye. Brooke's eyelids twitched at her mother's pronouncement. Kara whispered, "You know, I get a sense that Brooke can hear what we're saying."

"Maybe it would make it easier to say good-bye if she could," Mrs. Kelly said.

Kara flinched. "But maybe you don't have to."

"We have to face it, Kara. Brooke wouldn't want to live like this."

Sara said, "But it's so early. You heard what the doctor said. She might wake up! Have you really thought this through?"

Mrs. Kelly studied Sara. "Why do you ask?"

"Well, I believe if we give God this situation, He can take Brooke if He wants. But He may choose to give her back to us."

Mrs. Kelly turned her back to her daughter and lowered her voice. "That's what I'm afraid of. I'm not sure I want her back if she can't be normal."

Sara continued, "But God's big enough to do anything. Even if Brooke did have some sort of handicapping condition, she would still have value and worth. People with disabilities live happy lives just like anyone else."

Mrs. Kelly raised her eyebrows as Sara asked, "Have you considered the guilt that may hound you if you make the decision to end Brooke's life? You don't need it. Why not let God decide what to do?"

A nurse stuck her head into Brooke's cubicle. "Mrs. Kelly, someone is asking for you in the waiting room."

"Oh, will you excuse me?"

Sara apologized. "I need to go, too."

Mrs. Kelly turned to Kara. She said, "Please stay with Brooke. I'll be back in a minute."

You are the Alpha and the Omega. You are the first and the last. Although our lives are as brief gusts of wind that rustle the grass for an instant, You care for us. You know and care about our conceptions and our deaths. Help me respect the lives You've created, from the very new to the vibrant to the frail to the weak. Be in control of my passage through this world, and help me respect the passages of others.

Additional Scripture reading: Psalm 62:5–8

THE
LOOK

I, even I, am He who blots out
    your transgressions for My own sake;
And I will not remember your sins.
    —Isaiah 43:25

While machines swooshed and gurgled, Kara tiptoed to Brooke's side and reached for her hand. "Hi, Brooke, it's me, Kara Daniels. I know you can hear me."

Brooke's face remained expressionless as her chest rose and fell in mechanical rhythm.

"I know you're feeling bad about your baby. But what I said earlier is true. Your baby is in the arms of God."

Kara detected the flicker of eye movement beneath Brooke's eyelids.

"And God is big enough to forgive you."

Squeezing Brooke's hand, Kara said, "He loves you, Brooke. So much that He sent His Son to die for you.

"Brooke, you're not the only one who hasn't lived a perfect life. I've messed up, too. Everyone has."

Kara stroked Brooke's hair and continued. "There really is a heaven, Brooke. That's where your baby is. I don't know if it's your time to die. But I know you can't get to heaven on your own. You'll need God's forgiveness to get through the gates.

"Brooke, I can help you. I can tell you what to pray. If you can hear me, pray in your heart, 'Dear God, forgive me for the wrong I've done. Come into my life and be my King. Thank You for sending Your Son, Jesus, to die for my sins.'"

Studying Brooke's face, Kara said, "Brooke, if you prayed that prayer with me, could . . . could you open your eyes?"

Kara waited, holding her breath. For an instant, Brooke's eyes cracked into narrow slits, allowing a tear to run down the side of her face.

Forgetting the tubes and monitors, Kara hugged Brooke. "I love you, sister. You are in God's hands now."

Thank You for second chances. In fact, no matter how many times I mess up, You're there, ready to forgive me—forgetting my sin. Because of Your love for me, I don't want to do wrong. I want to live for You.

Additional Scripture reading: Acts 3:19–20

❖

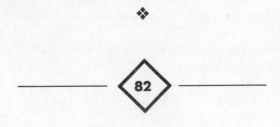

MATT'S RETURN

The LORD is good to those who
    wait for Him,
To the soul who seeks Him.
    —Lamentations 3:25

Later, when Mrs. Kelly had relieved Kara's bedside watch, Kara wandered into the waiting room.

When she pushed open the double doors, she started. Matt and Dee Ann were in the corner of the room involved in intimate conversation.

Dee Ann looked up and called, "Kara, how's Brooke?"

Kara sat on a seat next to the couple. "I'm not sure. She seems to be unconscious, although she can hear what you say to her. We had a long talk about God. I believe she asked Jesus into her heart!"

"That's wonderful! Isn't it, Matt?"

Matt nodded and grinned.

"So," Kara asked, "what's going on here? You two look happier today."

Matt bowed his head. "I was a real jerk last night, Kara. Dee Ann's news came as such a shock."

"So, how do you feel now?" Kara asked.

"I thought about it all night, and one thing kept coming back to me."

"What's that?"

"Dee Ann's character. It took a really great girl to stand up for her baby's life. I decided I was proud of her."

Smiling, Dee Ann said, "Kara and your mom helped. I didn't do it alone."

Matt put his arm around her. "I know, but still a lot of girls would have taken the easy way out."

"I've had my regrets about what's happened," Dee Ann confessed. "But I don't have any guilt. I know I'm clean before the Lord."

Kara nodded her head. "That's important, Dee." She faced Matt. "So is your relationship on again?"

"We're playing it by ear. Who's to say that Dee Ann and I will be together when this whole thing is over?"

Dee Ann smiled. "And who's to say we won't?"

"But," Kara asked, "what about your reputation, Matt?"

"That's tough," Matt admitted. "And to be honest, I'm still concerned. But I think the truth will come out. Not that I'm going to go around spreading gossip about Jack."

Dee Ann looked guilty. "I'm afraid I told most of the story when the police took my statement last night. Plus, I'm going down to the station this afternoon to press rape charges against Jack. I know I shouldn't have been drinking the night Jack raped me, but still, Jack stepped way out of line. I have to face the consequences of the rape with my pregnancy. Jack should have to face the rape's consequences with the law. How else will he understand that no means no?"

"Don't feel bad," Kara said. "I told the police about the rape, too. It helped them establish a motive for what they suspect was a vehicular assault." Turning, Kara smiled. "Matt, I'm so glad you came around. I can feel God's hand in this. I think the next few months should prove to be a real adventure indeed."

Thank You for Your goodness. Thank You for going before me and making my path straight. Sometimes it seems that life gets so complicated. But You help me sort out the issues. Give me power to live my life in such a way that I attract other people to Your love.

Additional Scripture reading: Lamentations 3:22–33

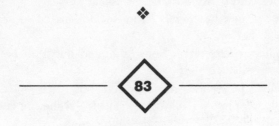

THE HEALING

Though He slay me, yet will I trust
   Him.—Job 13:15

Later that evening, Kara looked up to see Todd wander into the waiting room.

"Where is everyone?" he asked.

"Matt and Dee Ann went to supper, and Ryan's visiting Jenni."

"I heard that Jack was okay, but how are the girls?"

"They've moved Jenni out of ICU and upgraded her condition to stable. It looks like she's going to be fine."

"How's Brooke?"

Kara shook her head. "The last report was that it was touch and go."

Todd sank into a chair next to Kara. "I'm sorry to hear that."

Kara and Todd sat in silence, watching the hands of the waiting room clock push time forward.

They jumped when an overhead speaker buzzed. "Code Blue, ICU-B. Code Blue, ICU-B!" a frantic voice called.

Todd sat up, watching nurses, doctors, and technicians scurry a crash cart through the double doors. "What's happening?" he asked.

Kara grasped his hand. "Brooke's in cubicle B! Something must be wrong!"

After what seemed hours, the hospital emergency team began to drift out of the ICU.

"Is Brooke okay?" Kara asked a passing nurse.

The nurse shook her head. "I'm not authorized to say. You'll have to talk to her mom."

A few minutes later, Mrs. Kelly stumbled out from behind the doors.

Kara jumped to her feet and Todd followed.

Mrs. Kelly wept into a hanky. Kara asked, "Is she . . . is she . . ."

Gasping for air, Mrs. Kelly said, "She's gone."

Kara and Todd surrounded her with hugs. "I'm really sorry, Mrs. Kelly," Todd said. "Really sorry."

"I am, too," Kara agreed through her tears. "But at least, we know she's in a better place."

Mrs. Kelly looked up. "Do we?"

"She's with God, Mrs. Kelly. I'm sure of it."

"I've never thought much about death. I hope you're right, Kara," Mrs. Kelly agreed. "Please excuse me. I've got to go now. There are some calls I need to make."

Todd and Kara returned to their seats, listening to the silence.

Finally, Todd asked, "Is this what God wanted? He wanted Brooke to die?"

Kara pondered his question. "We did bind the Enemy and give God control of the situation."

Todd nodded his head. Kara continued, "And you know, I really believe that Brooke met God this afternoon. I also believe that tonight, she's healed. She's free, hugging her baby in heaven's beautiful flower garden."

"So that's what she meant. She did have an abortion."

Kara wiped her eyes. "Yes. But it's really sort of beautiful, you know? I'd almost be happy if I didn't feel such a loss."

"I know what you mean," Todd agreed. "But it helps to know she's found a better life."

Kara nodded and whispered, "Thank You, Jesus. I trust Brooke's soul to You."

Thank You that You are with us in life and that You've made a way for us to be with You in death. Help me to introduce my loved ones to You so their deaths will be not a tragic end but a beautiful beginning. Give me opportunities to ensure that my whole family finds Your love. I trust You, regardless of the cost.

Additional Scripture reading: 1 Corinthians 15:54–58

A NEW BEGINNING

When You said, "Seek My face,"
My heart said to You, "Your face,
LORD, I will seek."
—Psalm 27:8

The next morning, Kara felt strange to be caught up in the hustle of getting ready for classes. She slipped into her T-shirt and jeans, then joined her family at the breakfast table.

Her dad studied her. "How are you feeling, Kara?"

"Okay, I guess," she said, pouring milk onto her bowl of cereal. "I'll feel even better after the funeral tomorrow."

Mrs. Daniels joined the family. "You and Matt have been through quite an ordeal."

Kara nodded her head as the family grasped hands in a circle of prayer.

Mr. Daniels prayed, "Lord, thank You for helping my children be bold in their stand for You. Bless them and honor their efforts. In Jesus' name."

Kara peeked at Matt from under her bangs. These first weeks had been hard, harder than she could have imagined. But through it all, God had been faithful.

Matt met her gaze as she lifted her spoon to her lips. He said, "So, little sis, it's good to see you eating again. You've really made a lot of progress."

Nodding, Kara said, "Yes. I'm off that stupid diet. But the best thing that's happened to me is the fact I don't have to walk in my faith alone. I've got good Christian friends who are walking with me."

Smiling, Matt said, "You do now. I wasn't so sure how your friendships were going for a while. You seemed to be headed in the wrong direction. But you turned things around by making the right choices. You really grew."

Kara smiled back. "I hate to admit it, but some of your advice was right on. It really helped."

Matt said, "I'm glad."

"Me, too," Kara agreed. "But now that I've grown, it will be exciting to see what adventures God has in store for me. I'm ready to move on . . . in Him.

Thank You that I can trust You. Sometimes the way is rough, but You're there, holding my hand. Thank You for honoring me with Your love and protection. Help me stay true to You and seek Your face so I can continue in my adventure with You.

Additional Scripture reading: Psalm 25:4–10

❖